Meeting SEN
in the Curriculum:
PE/SPORT

Other titles in the Meeting SEN in the Curriculum series:

Meeting Special Needs in English
Tim Hurst
1 84312 157 3

Meeting Special Needs in Maths
Brian Sharp
1 84312 158 1

Meeting Special Needs in Modern Foreign Languages
Sally McKeown
1 84312 165 4

Meeting Special Needs in Citizenship
Alan Combes
1 84312 169 7

Meeting Special Needs in Religious Education
Dilwyn Hunt
1 84312 167 0

Meeting Special Needs in History
Richard Harris and Ian Luff
1 84312 163 8

Meeting Special Needs in Design and Technology
Louise Davies
1 84312 166 2

Meeting Special Needs in Art
Kim Earle and Gill Curry
1 84312 161 1

Meeting Special Needs in Music
Victoria Jacquiss and Diane Paterson
1 84312 168 9

Meeting Special Needs in ICT
Mike North and Sally McKeown
1 84312 160 3

Meeting Special Needs in Science
Carol Holden
1 84312 159 X

Meeting Special Needs in Geography
Diane Swift
1 84312 162 X

Meeting SEN
in the Curriculum:
PE/SPORT

Crispin Andrews

 David Fulton Publishers

David Fulton Publishers Ltd
The Chiswick Centre, 414 Chiswick High Road, London W4 5TF

www.fultonpublishers.co.uk

First published in Great Britain in 2005 by David Fulton Publishers

10   9   8   7   6   5   4   3   2   1

David Fulton Publishers is a division of Granada Learning, part of ITV plc.

British Library Cataloguing in Publication Data
A catalogue record for this book is available from the British Library.

ISBN 1 84312 164 6

Typeset by Servis Filmsetting Ltd, Manchester
Printed and bound in Great Britain

Contents

Foreword

All young people have the right to enjoy and benefit from a high-quality experience in PE and sport. However, meeting the needs of students with special educational needs is not always that straightforward and we need to continue to challenge ourselves to ensure not only an appropriate PE curriculum, but also access to sport and physical activities outside of school hours and linked to wider opportunities. Through tailoring the activity and the environment to the needs of the individual, many of the existing barriers to participation and engagement can be overcome.

Solutions are out there; around the country many schools are getting to grips with the issues involved in facilitating access to PE and sport for all. Case studied within this book, much can be learnt from the inclusive approaches being developed by these schools and their partners. Not only have innovative, curricular and out-of-school hours learning opportunities been designed, but learning environments – both in terms of physical characteristics and departmental ethos – have also been modified. Other schools have got to grips with those crucial enabling factors of school organisation that allow inclusive approaches to PE and sport to be effective.

The Youth Sport Trust is committed to the dissemination of good practice, and the practical, case study-driven nature of this book makes it an ideal contributor to this process. One of its many strengths is that it does not treat the subject in isolation. Most teachers must meet the needs of students with special educational needs within a mainstream setting, where the needs of all children must be taken into account, and the advice contained within these pages reflects this reality. Solutions to common difficulties and barriers faced by teachers in the development of an inclusive approach are also provided.

I am certain that the practical advice and real-life case studies contained within this book will help practitioners develop their own successful inclusive approaches that meet the needs of all students, including those with special educational needs.

Steve Grainger
Chief Executive, Youth Sport Trust

May 2005

Acknowledgements

I would like to extend my grateful thanks to the many colleagues who have been generous with their time and expertise in providing me with information, ideas and encouragement for this book:

Debbie Ashford – DfES

Ros Bastian – Partnership Development Manager, Penryn College, Cornwall

Mark Botterill – Inclusion Officer Youth Sport Trust

Jason Bridges – Head of PE – Ninestiles School, Birmingham

Ian Broadbridge – DfES

David Bullas – Director of Sport – Dayncourt School, Nottingham

Di Caesar – Advisory Teacher SEN – Gloucestershire County Council

Sue Campbell – Chief Executive, Youth Sport Trust

Crichton Casbon – Lead Consultant for PE with the QCA

Anne Craddock – Disability Sports Consultant

Mike Diaper – Director of the PESSCL project, DfES/DCMS

Katie Donovan – International Development Director, GISA

Lorraine Everard, Partnership Development Manager, Bexley School Sport Partnership

Steve Grainger – Managing Director, Youth Sport Trust

Carol Halpin – Inside Out Project Officer, Nottinghamshire County Council

Emma Hughes – Press Officer, QCA

Marie Hunter – Head teacher, Penryn College, Cornwall

Felicity Halsey – SENCO, Kingshill School, Cirencester

Simon Harris – Head of PE, Wilson Stuart Special School, Birmingham

Angela Jamcs – Advisory teacher for PE, Gloucestershire County Council

Mike Johnson – Penryn College, Cornwall

Richard Little – Director of Sport, Eltham Green School, London

Jane McKay – School Sport Co-ordinator – Castlegreen Special School, Sunderland

Alison Philpott – Partnership Development Manager, Redbridge Community College, Southampton

Carole Raymond – Specialist Adviser for PE, Ofsted

Anna Robinson – Director of Sport, Hailsham Community College, East Sussex

Lynne Spackman – QCA consultant

Steve Spiers – Sports Development Officer, South Gloucestershire Council

Alistair Symondson – *Cricket World* magazine

Jane Tompkins – *Cricket World* magazine

Donna Tipping – Press and Publications Officer, Youth Sport Trust

Dave Tromans – Director of Sport, Knottingley High School, West Yorkshire

Rob Watson – PE/SENCO – The Valley Comprehensive, Nottinghamshire

Tony Willard – EYES Project Co-ordinator, Aylesbury Vale District Council

Richard Whitehead – Teaching Assistant, Dayncourt School, Nottingham

Doug Williamson – Nottingham Trent University

Contributors to the Series

The author

Crispin Andrews is an educational sports journalist. Over the last five years he has written extensively on a wide variety of issues within this genre – contributing regularly to the *TES, Teachers* magazine, both the primary and secondary editions, *SecEd, PE and Sport Today, Special Children* and many others. He is also community correspondent for *Cricket World* magazine. A qualified teacher, Crispin is a practising sports coach, regularly coaching cricket and football in schools in and around Aylesbury, Buckinghamshire. He has also developed sporting opportunities for local girls to play both sports.

Series editor

Alan Combes started teaching in South Yorkshire in 1967 and was Head of English at several secondary schools before taking on the role of Head of PSHE as part of being senior teacher at Pindar School, Scarborough. He took early retirement to focus on his writing career and has authored two citizenship textbooks as well as writing several features for the *TES*. He has been used as an adviser on citizenship by the DfES and has emphasised citizenship's importance for pupils with special educational needs as a speaker for NASEN.

A dedicated team of SEN specialists and subject specialists have contributed to the *Meeting Special Needs in the Curriculum* series.

SEN specialists

Sue Briggs is a freelance education consultant based in Hereford. She writes and speaks on inclusion, special educational needs and disability, and Autistic Spectrum Disorders, and is a lay member of the SEN and Disability Tribunal. Until recently, she was SEN Inclusion Co-ordinator for Herefordshire Education Directorate. Originally trained as a secondary music teacher, Sue has extensive experience in mainstream and special schools. For six years she was teacher in charge of a language disorder unit.

Sue Cunningham is a learning support co-ordinator at a large mainstream secondary school in the West Midlands, where she manages a large team of Learning Support teachers and assistants. She has experience of working in both mainstream and special schools and has set up and managed a resource base for pupils with moderate learning difficulties in the mainstream as part of an initiative to promote a more inclusive education for pupils with SEN.

Sally McKeown works in the inclusion team at BECTa and is a consultant for a number of other organisations including Network Training, NIACE and LSDA. She is also a freelance journalist and writes regularly for the *TES*, *Guardian* and *Special Children* magazines. Sally is author of *Unlocking Potential* and co-author of *Supporting Children with Dyslexia* (Questions Publishing).

Subject specialists

Maths

Brian Sharp is a Key Stage 3 mathematics consultant for Herefordshire. Brian has a long experience of working both in special and mainstream schools as a teacher of mathematics. He has a range of management experience, including SENCO, mathematics and ICT co-ordinator.

English

Tim Hurst has been a special educational needs co-ordinator in five schools and is particularly interested in the role and use of language in teaching.

Science

Carol Holden is a science teacher and assistant SENCO in a mainstream secondary school. She has developed courses for pupils with SEN within science and has a graduate diploma and MA in Educational Studies, focusing on SEN.

History

Richard Harris has been teaching since 1989. He has taught in three comprehensive schools, as history teacher, Head of Department and Head of Faculty. He has worked as teacher consultant for secondary history in Berkshire.

Ian Luff is assistant headteacher of Kesgrave High School, Suffolk and has been Head of History in three comprehensive schools.

Design & Technology

Louise T. Davies is part-time Principal Officer for Design and Technology at the Qualifications and Curriculum Authority and also a freelance consultant. She is an experienced presenter and author of award-winning resources and books for schools. She chairs the Special Needs Advisory Group for the Design and Technology Association.

Music

Victoria Jaquiss is SEN Specialist for Music for children with emotional and behavioural difficulties in Leeds. She devised a system of musical notation primarily for use with steel pans, for which, in 2002, she was awarded the fellowship of the Royal Society of Arts.

Diane Paterson works as an inclusive music curriculum teacher in Leeds.

Geography

Diane Swift is a project leader for the Geographical Association. Her interest in special needs developed whilst she was a geography adviser and inspector.

Art

Kim Earle is Able Pupils Consultant for St Helens and has been a Head of art and design. Kim is also a practising designer jeweller.

Gill Curry is Gifted and Talented Strand Co-ordinator for the Wirral. She has twenty years' experience as Head of art and has also been an art advisory teacher. She is also a practising artist specialising in print.

Religious education

Dilwyn Hunt has worked as a specialist RE adviser, first in Birmingham and now in Dudley. He has a wide range of experience in the teaching of RE including mainstream and special RE.

ICT

Mike North works for ICTC, an independent consultancy specialising in the effective use of ICT in education. He develops educational materials and provides advice and support for the SEN sector.

Sally McKeown is an Education Officer with Becta, the government funded agency responsible for managing the National Grid for Learning and the FERL website. She is responsible for the use of IT for learners with disabilities, learning difficulties or additional needs.

Citizenship

Alan Combes started teaching in South Yorkshire in 1967 and was Head of English at several secondary schools before taking on the role of Head of PSHE as part of being senior teacher at Pindar School, Scarborough. He took early retirement to focus on his writing career and has authored two citizenship text-books as well as writing several features for the *TES*. He has been used as an adviser on citizenship by the DfES and has emphasised citizenship's importance for special needs pupils as a speaker for NASEN.

Modern foreign languages

Sally McKeown is responsible for language-based work in the Inclusion team at Becta. She has a particular interest in learning difficulties and dyslexia. She writes regularly for the *TES, Guardian* and *Special Children* magazine.

Contents of the CD

The CD contains a variety of templates and checklists which can be amended as appropriate and printed out for use by the purchasing institution. The resources for pupils, e.g. self-evaluation checklist, rules for sports activities may be made more accessible by enlarging the print, double spacing, etc. and changing the background colour. Alternatively, print onto pastel-coloured paper for ease of reading.

1. INSET Activity 1 – What Do We Really Think?
2. INSET Activity 2 – SEN and Disability Act 2001 (SENDA)
3. Assessment/Self-evaluation Checklists, Based on the Indicators of High Quality PE and Sport
4. Evaluating Quality Provision
5. High Quality PE and Sport: Individual Checklist (SEN)
6. Strategic Planner
7. Strategic Planner Template
8. P Scales
9. Individual Education Plans (Source: The Valley Comprehensive School, Notts)
10. Unit of Work: Striking and Fielding
11. Unit of Work: Table Cricket
12. Unit of Work: Football
13. Unit of Work: Aiming Games
14. Unit of Work: Template
15. Accessing Funding
16. Accessing Funding: Template
17. Press Release Template
18. Polybat
19. Table Cricket
20. Target Cricket
21. Zone Hockey
22. Floor Lacrosse

The author and publishers would like to thank Doug Williamson, Nottingham Trent University, and the Youth Sports Trust for allowing the copying of the rules and instructions for the adapted games (Table cricket, Target cricket, Zone hockey and Floor lacrosse.

Introduction

All children have the right to a good education and the opportunity to fulfil their potential. All teachers should expect to teach children with special educational needs (SEN) and all schools should play their part in educating children from the local community, whatever their background or ability. *Removing Barriers to Achievement: The Government's Strategy for SEN* (DfES 2004)

A raft of legislation and statutory guidance over the past few years has sought to make our mainstream education system more inclusive and ensure that pupils with a diverse range of ability and need are well catered for. This means that all staff need to have an awareness of how children learn and develop in different ways and an understanding of how barriers to achievement can be removed – or at least minimised.

These barriers often result from inappropriate teaching styles, inaccessible teaching materials or ill-advised grouping of pupils, as much as from an individual child's physical, sensory or cognitive impairments: a fact which is becoming better understood. It is this developing understanding that is now shaping the legislative and advisory landscape of our education system, and making it necessary for all teachers to reconsider carefully their curriculum planning and classroom practice.

The major statutory requirements and non-statutory guidance are summarised in Chapter 1, setting the context for this resource and providing useful starting points for departmental INSET.

It is clear that provision for pupils with special educational needs (SEN) is not the sole responsibility of the Special Educational Needs Co-ordinator (SENCO) and his/her team of assistants. If, in the past, subject teachers have 'taken a back seat' in the planning and delivery of a suitable curriculum for these children and expected the Learning Support department to bridge the gap between what was on offer in the gym or on the sports field and what they actually needed – they can no longer do so. The *Code of Practice* (2002) states.

All teaching and non teaching staff should be involved in the development of the school's SEN policy and be fully aware of the school's procedure for identifying, assessing and making provision for pupils with SEN.

Chapter 2 looks at departmental policy for SEN provision and provides useful audit material for use by PE staff in reviewing and developing current practice.

The term 'special educational needs' is now widely used and has become something of a catch-all descriptor – rendering it less than useful in many cases. Before the Warnock Report (1978) and subsequent introduction of the term 'special educational needs', any pupils who, for whatever reason, (cognitive difficulties, emotional and behavioural difficulties, speech and language disorders) progressed more slowly than the 'norm' were designated 'remedials' and grouped together in the bottom sets, without the benefit in many cases, of specialist subject teachers.

But the SEN tag was also applied to pupils in special schools who had more significant needs and had previously been identified as 'disabled' or even 'uneducable'. Add to these the deaf pupils, those with impaired vision, others with mobility problems, and even children from other countries, with a limited understanding of the English language – who may or may not have been highly intelligent – and you have a recipe for confusion, to say the least.

The day-to-day descriptors used in the staffroom are gradually being moderated and refined as greater knowledge and awareness of special needs is built up. (We still hear staff describing pupils as 'totally thick', a 'nutcase' or 'complete moron' – but hopefully only as a means of letting off steam!) However, there are terms in common use which, though more measured and well-meaning, can still be unhelpful and misleading. Teachers will describe a child as being 'dyslexic' when they mean that he is poor at reading and writing, 'ADHD' has become a synonym for badly behaved, and a child who seems to be withdrawn or just eccentric is increasingly described as 'autistic'.

The whole process of applying labels is fraught with danger, but sharing a common vocabulary – and more importantly, a common understanding – can help colleagues to express their concerns about a pupil and address the issues as they appear in the gym or on the sports field. Often, this is better achieved by identifying the particular areas of difficulty experienced by the pupil rather than by puzzling over what syndrome he may have. The Code of Practice identifies four main areas of difficulty and these are detailed in Chapter 3 – along with an 'at a glance' guide to a wide range of syndromes and conditions, and guidance on how they might present barriers to learning.

There is no doubt that the number of children with special needs being educated in mainstream schools is growing:

> . . . because of the increased emphasis on the inclusion of children with SEN in mainstream schools the number of these children is increasing, as are the severity and variety of their SEN. Children with a far wider range of learning difficulties and variety of medical conditions, as well as sensory difficulties and physical disabilities, are now attending mainstream classes. The implication of this is that mainstream school teachers need to expand their knowledge and skills with regard to the needs of children with SEN. (Stakes and Hornby 2000:3)

The continuing move to greater inclusion means that PE teachers can now expect to teach pupils with varied, and quite significant special educational needs at some time. Even five years ago, it was rare to come across children with Asperger's/Down's/Tourette's Syndrome, Autistic Spectrum Disorder or significant physical/sensory disabilities in community secondary schools. Now, they are entering mainstream education in growing numbers and there is a realisation that their 'inclusion' cannot be simply the responsibility of the SENCO and support staff. All staff have to be aware of particular learning needs and able to employ strategies in the classroom, gym and swimming pool that directly address those needs.

Chapter 4 considers the components of an inclusive environment for teaching PE and sport and how physical features and resources, the structure of the lesson and teaching approaches can make a real difference to pupils with special needs. This theme is extended in Chapter 5 to look more closely at teaching and learning styles and consider ways in which to help all pupils maximise their potential.

The monitoring of pupils' achievements and progress is a key factor in identifying and meeting their learning needs. Those pupils who make slower progress than their peers are often working just as hard, or even harder, but their efforts can go unrewarded. Chapter 6 addresses the importance of target setting and subsequent assessment and review in acknowledging pupils' achievements and in showing the department's effectiveness in value-added terms.

Liaising with the SENCO and support staff is an important part of every teacher's role. The SENCO's status in a secondary school often means that this teacher is part of the leadership team and influential in shaping whole school policy and practice. Specific duties might include:

- ensuring liaison with parents and other professionals;

- advising and supporting teaching and support staff;

- ensuring that appropriate Individual Education Plans are in place;

- ensuring that relevant background information about individual children with special educational needs is collected, recorded and updated;

- making plans for future support and setting targets for improvement;

- monitoring and reviewing action taken.

The SENCO has invariably undergone training in different aspects of special needs provision and has much to offer colleagues in terms of in-house training and advice about appropriate materials to use with pupils. The SENCO should be a frequent and valuable point of reference for all staff, but is often overlooked in this capacity. The presence of the SENCO at the occasional departmental meeting can be very effective in developing teachers' skills in relation to meeting SEN, making them aware of new initiatives and methodology and sharing information about individual children.

In most schools, however, the SENCO's skills and knowledge are channelled to the chalkface via a team of Teaching or Learning Support Assistants (TAs, LSAs). These assistants can be very able and well-qualified, but very underused by staff in the PE department, beyond helping pupils to get changed. Chapter 7 looks at how teachers can manage support in a way that makes the best use of a valuable resource.

The revised regulations for SEN provision make it clear that mainstream schools are expected to provide for pupils with a wide diversity of needs, and teaching is evaluated on the extent to which all pupils are engaged and enabled to achieve. This book has been produced in response to the implications of all of this for secondary teachers of PE and sport. It has been written by a subject specialist with support from colleagues who have expertise within the SEN field so that the information and guidance given is both subject specific and pedagogically sound. The book and accompanying CD provide a resource that can be used with colleagues:

- to shape departmental policy and practice for special needs provision;

- to enable staff to react with a measured response when inclusion issues arise;

- to ensure that every pupil achieves appropriately in PE and sport.

CHAPTER 1

Meeting Special Educational Needs – Your Responsibility

Everyone can climb a mountain. We just need to make sure that we give each person the right mountain to climb and value everyone's achievements. (Frank Dick OBE, President of the European Athletics Coaches Association)

When Frank Dick included this statement in his speech to delegates at the Youth Sport Trust's Conference in October 2004, he was reinforcing the philosophy of inclusion that has become a major issue in much of the educational legislation and government guidance emerging at the start of the twenty-first century. This chapter reviews the contributions made to the 'inclusion movement' by the authorities.

The Index for Inclusion (Vaughan 2000) states that 'inclusion in education involves the process of increasing the participation of students in, and reducing their exclusion from, the cultures, curricula and communities of local schools.' It was distributed to all maintained schools by the Department for Education and Skills and has been a valuable tool for many schools as they have worked to develop their inclusive practice. It supports

Photo: Simon Harris

schools in the review of their policies, practices and procedures, and the development of an inclusive approach, and where it has been used as part of the school improvement process – looking at inclusion in the widest sense – it has been a great success. For many people, however, *The Index* lacked any real teeth, and recent legislation and non-statutory guidance is more authoritative.

The SEN and Disability Act 2001

The SEN and Disability Act 2001 amended the Disability Discrimination Act 1995 and created important new duties for schools:

- to take reasonable steps to ensure that disabled pupils are not placed at a substantial disadvantage in relation to the education and other services they provide. This means they must anticipate where barriers to learning lie and take action to remove them as far as they are able. In the case of PE, these could be physical barriers, such as access to changing rooms and playing areas, issues relating to the appropriateness of the tasks and activities being set, or even a lack of awareness amongst staff of how to meet the needs of students with special educational needs in PE.

- to plan strategically to increase the extent to which disabled pupils can participate in the curriculum. In an age of inter-agency partnership and inter-school collaboration, every child is at the centre of a multi-layered learning environment. Within it the actions and attitudes of all: from teacher to department, school management to LEA, regional to national policy makers, will impinge to varying degrees upon the nature of that environment and its suitability for a particular child. While the PE teacher sets out the learning objectives and activities within a lesson or module, what they teach and how they teach it will be influenced by departmental policy and the values of the head of PE. Similarly, where PE and sport is valued as a high-profile part of a school, with the full support of school management and head teacher, it is far easier for a PE department to be innovative in its organisation and delivery of curricular and out-of-school hours learning opportunities. An LEA which values and supports inclusive practice and PE & sport is more likely to encourage schools to mirror that ethos, and at national level, the current government's support for both encourages a higher profile for both inclusion and PE/sport. To develop a truly inclusive learning environment, the role of all of the above is crucial. Therefore, planning for SEN provision in conjunction with a host of outside bodies – all of whom can offer advice, assistance and opportunities for youngsters – is advisable. Schools inside School Sport Partnerships should be able to access these networks through their Partnership Development Manager and, for those outside, the local council's sports development department is usually a good first port of call. Give them an idea of the issues being faced and, even if they can't help themselves, they should be able to facilitate contact with an organisation that can.

The reasonable steps taken might include:

- changing policies and practices

- changing course requirements

- changing the physical features of a building or facility

- providing interpreters or other support workers

- delivering courses in alternative ways

- providing materials in other formats

The Revised National Curriculum

The Revised National Curriculum (2002) emphasises the provision of effective learning opportunities for all learners, and establishes three principles for promoting inclusion:

- setting suitable learning challenges

- responding to pupils' diverse learning needs

- overcoming potential barriers to learning and assessment

The National Curriculum guidance suggests that staff may need to differentiate tasks and materials, and facilitate access to learning by:

- encouraging pupils to use all available senses and experiences

- planning for participation in all activities

- helping children to manage their behaviour, take part in learning and prepare for work

- helping pupils to manage their emotions

- giving teachers, where necessary, the discretion to teach pupils material from earlier key stages, providing consideration is given to age-appropriate learning contexts. For instance, the Youth Sport Trust's revised TOPs cards, designed for use with Key Stage 2 pupils are an ideal resource to help meet the needs of children with SEN at secondary school. A host of differentiated activities for all

Photo: Simon Harris

areas of the PE curriculum are provided in a colourfully illustrated, easily accessible format. Unfortunately, these cards are not generally available and can only be accessed by schools and teachers taking part in training. Contact the local Partnership Development Manager or LEA PE adviser to find out which nearby primary schools have done the training and might possess the resources.

The Qualifications and Curriculum Authority (QCA) have also introduced performance descriptions (P levels/P scales) to enable teachers to observe and record small steps of progress made by some pupils with SEN. These descriptions outline early learning and attainment for each subject in the National Curriculum, including Citizenship, RE and PSHE. They chart progress up to NC level 1 through eight steps. The performance descriptions for P1 to P3 are common across all subjects and outline the types and range of general performance that some pupils with learning difficulties might characteristically demonstrate. From level P4 onwards, many believe it is possible to describe performance in a way that indicates the emergence of subject-focused skills, knowledge and understanding. (Read more about this in Chapter 6.)

The Code of Practice for Special Educational Needs

The Revised Code of Practice (implemented in 2002) describes a cyclical process of planning, target setting and review for pupils with special educational needs. It also makes clear the expectation that the vast majority of pupils with special needs will be educated in mainstream settings. Those identified as needing over and above what the school can provide from its own resources, however, are nominated for 'School Action Plus', and outside agencies will be involved in planned intervention. This may involve professionals from the Learning Support Service, a specialist teacher or therapist, or an educational psychologist, working with the school's SENCO to put together an Individual Education Plan (IEP) for the pupil. In a minority of cases (the numbers vary widely between LEAs) pupils may be assessed by a multi-disciplinary team on behalf of the local education authority, whose representatives then decide whether or not to issue a statement of SEN. This is a legally binding document detailing the child's needs and setting out the resources which should be provided. It is reviewed every year.

FUNDAMENTAL PRINCIPLES OF THE SPECIAL NEEDS CODE OF PRACTICE:

- A child with special educational needs should have their needs met.
- The special educational needs of children will normally be met in mainstream schools or settings.
- The views of the child should be sought and taken into account.
- Parents have a vital role to play in supporting their child's education.
- Children with special educational needs should be offered full access to a broad, balanced and relevant education, including an appropriate curriculum for the foundation stage and the National Curriculum.

Ofsted

Ofsted inspectors are required to make judgements about a school's inclusion policy, and how this is translated into practice in individual classrooms. According to Ofsted (2003) the following key factors help schools to become more inclusive:

- a climate of acceptance of all pupils

- careful preparation of placements for SEN pupils

- availability of sufficient suitable teaching and personal support

- widespread awareness among staff of the particular needs of SEN pupils and an understanding of the practical ways of meeting these needs in the classroom

- sensitive allocation to teaching groups and careful curriculum modification, timetables and social arrangements

- availability of appropriate materials and teaching aids and adapted accommodation

- an active approach to personal and social development, as well as to learning

- well-defined and consistently applied approaches to managing difficult behaviour

- assessment, recording and reporting procedures which can embrace and express adequately the progress of pupils with more complex SEN who make only small gains in learning and PSD

- involving parents/carers as fully as possible in decision-making, keeping them well informed about their child's progress and giving them as much practical support as possible

- developing and taking advantage of training opportunities, including links with special schools and other schools

Carole Raymond, an Ofsted specialist adviser for PE, states:

In general, schools need to provide more evidence that the needs of pupils with SEN are being addressed through the utilisation of a range of approaches and strategies. Often the fear of appearing 'unsatisfactory' in the eyes of an inspector makes teachers reluctant to take risks and encourages them to rely on tried and trusted methods of delivery. Yet if progression is to be for all children, we must challenge traditional practices and search for new and better ways of engaging larger numbers of children in PE and sport.

Policy into practice

Effective teaching for pupils with special educational needs is, by and large, effective for all pupils, but as schools become more inclusive, teachers need to be able to respond to a wider range of needs. The Government's strategy for SEN (*Removing Barriers to Learning,* (DfES 2004)) sets out ambitious proposals to 'help teachers expand their repertoire of inclusive skills and strategies and plan confidently to include children with increasingly complex needs'.

In many cases, pupils' individual needs will be met through greater differentiation of tasks and materials, i.e. school-based intervention as set out in the SEN Code of Practice. A smaller number of pupils may need access to specialist equipment and approaches or to alternative or adapted activities, as part of a School Action Plus programme, augmented by advice and support from external specialists. The QCA, on its 2003 website encouraged teachers to take specific action to provide access to learning for pupils with special educational needs by:

(a) providing for pupils who need help with communication, language and literacy, through:

- using texts that pupils can read and understand

- using visual and written materials in different formats, including large print, symbol text and Braille

- using ICT, other technological aids and taped materials

- using alternative and augmentative communication, including signs and symbols

- using translators, communicators and amanuenses

(b) planning, where necessary, to develop pupils' understanding through the use of all available senses and experiences by:

- using materials and resources that pupils can access through sight, touch, sound, taste or smell

- using word descriptions and other stimuli to make up for a lack of first-hand experiences

- using ICT, visual and other materials to increase pupils' knowledge of the wider world

- encouraging pupils to take part in everyday activities such as play, drama, class visits and exploring the environment

(c) planning for pupils' full participation in learning and in physical and practical activities by:

- using specialist aids and equipment

- providing support from adults or peers when needed

- adapting tasks or environments

- providing alternative activities, where necessary.

(d) helping pupils to manage their behaviour, to take part in learning effectively and safely, and, at Key Stage 4, to prepare for work by:

- setting realistic demands and stating them explicitly

- using positive behaviour management, including a clear structure of rewards and sanctions

- giving pupils every chance and encouragement to develop the skills they need to work well with a partner or a group

- teaching pupils to value and respect the contribution of others

- encouraging and teaching independent working skills

- teaching essential safety rules

(e) helping individuals to manage their emotions, particularly trauma or stress, and to take part in learning by:

- identifying aspects of learning in which the pupil will engage and plan short-term, easily achievable goals in selected activities

- providing positive feedback to reinforce and encourage learning and build self-esteem

- selecting tasks and materials sensitively to avoid unnecessary stress for the pupil

- creating a supportive learning environment in which the pupil feels safe and is able to engage with learning

- allowing time for the pupil to engage with learning and gradually increasing the range of activities and demands

The QCA has also been involved in a detailed investigation into PE and school sport. Working with a number of schools, it has piloted numerous projects – each looking at ways in which PE and sport can be used to assist wider learning and development. Details can be found at www.qca.org.uk/pess

Pupils with disabilities

The QCA goes on to provide guidance on pupils with disabilities, pointing out that not all pupils with disabilities will necessarily have special educational needs. Many learn alongside their peers with little need for additional resources beyond the aids which they use as part of their daily life, such as a wheelchair, a hearing aid or equipment to aid vision. Teachers' planning must ensure, however, that these pupils are enabled to participate as fully and effectively as possible in the curriculum by:

- planning appropriate amounts of time to allow for the satisfactory completion of tasks. This might involve:

  - taking account of the very slow pace at which some pupils will be able to record work, either manually or with specialist equipment, and of the physical effort required

  - being aware of the high levels of concentration necessary for some pupils when following or interpreting text or graphics, particularly when using vision aids or tactile methods, and of the tiredness which may result

  - being aware of the effort required by some pupils to follow oral work, whether through use of residual hearing, lip reading or a signer, and of the tiredness or loss of concentration which may occur

- planning opportunities, where necessary, for the development of skills in practical aspects of the curriculum. This might involve:

  - providing adapted, modified or alternative activities or approaches to learning in PE and ensuring that these have integrity and equivalence to the National Curriculum and enable pupils to make appropriate progress

  - providing alternative or adapted activities for pupils who are unable to manipulate equipment or materials

  - ensuring that all pupils can be included and participate safely in PE and sport activities

- identifying aspects of Programmes of Study and attainment targets that may present specific difficulties for individuals. This might involve:

  - providing opportunities for pupils to develop strength in depth where they cannot meet the particular requirements of a subject – particularly in relation to movement

  - discounting these aspects in appropriate individual cases when required to make a judgement against level descriptions

Summary

Pupils with a wide range of needs – physical/sensory, emotional, cognitive and social – are present in increasing numbers, in all mainstream settings. Government policy points the way, with inclusion at the forefront of national policy – but it is up to teachers to make the rhetoric a reality. Teachers are ultimately responsible for all the children they teach. In terms of participation, achievement, enjoyment – the buck stops with them.

CHAPTER 2

Departmental Policy

It is crucial that departmental policy describes a strategy for meeting pupils' special educational needs. The policy should set the scene for any visitor to the PE department – from supply staff to inspectors – and make a valuable contribution to the departmental handbook. The process of developing a department SEN policy offers the opportunity to clarify and evaluate current thinking and practice within the PE team and to establish a consistent approach.

The policy should:

- clarify the responsibilities of all staff and identify any with specialist training and/or knowledge

- describe the curriculum on offer and how it can be differentiated

- outline arrangements for assessment and reporting

- guide staff on how to work effectively with support staff

- identify staff training

The starting point will be the school's SEN policy as required by the Education Act 1996, with each subject department 'fleshing out' the detail in a way which describes how things work in practice. The writing of a policy should be much more than a paper exercise completed to satisfy the senior management team and Ofsted inspectors: it is an opportunity for staff to come together as a team and create a framework for teaching PE in a way that makes it accessible to all pupils in the school.

Where to start when writing a policy

Schools inside School Sport Partnerships are required to undergo general audits to identify strengths and weaknesses, gaps in provision and areas for development. Although they will not have a school sport co-ordinator to lead this process, there is no reason why those outside the current network of partnerships should not also undertake a similar process. This audit should take the needs of all pupils into consideration and can act as a starting point for reviewing current policy on SEN provision or informing the writing of a new policy. It will involve gathering information and reviewing current practice with regard to pupils with SEN, and is best completed by the whole of the department, preferably with some additional advice from the SENCO or another member of staff with responsibility for SEN. An audit carried out by the whole department can provide a valuable opportunity for professional development if it is seen as an exercise in sharing good practice and encouraging joint planning. But before embarking on an audit, it is worth investing some time in a department meeting or training day, to raise awareness of special educational needs legislation and to establish a shared philosophy.

Again it should be stressed that undertaking any such analysis in isolation would be foolish. A vast amount of expertise exists outside of school. In the LEA advisory service, special schools – even in the local offices of national governing bodies of sport – there are people who may be able to advise on the desirability and usefulness of various strategies. Some local authority sports development departments now have disability sports officers. With a variety of perspectives and backgrounds, all these individuals may help schools challenge existing assumptions and come up with innovative new solutions.

Appendix 2 contains an activity to use with staff. (These are also on the accompanying CD as OHT layouts, with additional exercises you may choose to use.)

The following headings may be useful in establishing a working policy:

General statement

- What does legislation and DfES guidance say?
- What does the school policy state?
- What do members of the department have to do to comply with it?
- Which partners have been involved?

Definition of SEN

- What does SEN mean?
- What are the areas of need and the categories used in the Code of Practice?
- Are there any special implications within the subject area?

Provision for staff within the department

- How is information shared?
- Who has responsibility for SEN within the department?

- How and when is information shared?

- Where and what information is stored?

Provision for pupils with SEN

- How are pupils with SEN assessed and monitored in the department?

- How are contributions to IEPs and reviews made?

- What criteria are used for organising teaching groups?

- What alternative courses are offered to pupils with SEN?

- What special internal and external examination arrangements are made?

- What guidance is available for working with support staff?

Resources and learning materials

- Is there any specialist equipment used in the department?

- How are resources developed?

- Where are resources stored?

- Are resources (including human resources) brought in from outside the school?

Staff Qualifications and Continuing Professional Development needs

- What qualifications do the members of the department have?

- What training has taken place?

- How is training planned?

- Is a record kept of training completed and training needs?

Monitoring and reviewing the policy

- How will the policy be monitored?

- When will the policy be reviewed?

The content of an SEN departmental policy

This section gives detailed information on what an SEN policy might include. Each heading is expanded with some detailed information and raises the main issues with regard to teaching pupils with SEN. At the end of each section there is an example statement. The example statements can be personalised and brought together to make a policy.

General statement with reference to the school's SEN policy

All schools must have an SEN policy according to the Education Act 1996. This policy will set out basic information on the school's SEN provision, how the school identifies, assesses and provides for pupils with SEN, including information on staffing and working in partnership with other professionals and parents.

Any department policy needs to have reference to the school SEN policy.

Example

> All members of the department will ensure that the needs of all pupils with SEN are met, according to the aims of the school and its SEN policy.

Definition of SEN

It is useful to insert at least the four areas of SEN in the department policy, as used in the Code of Practice for Special Educational Needs. It is also useful to remember that children with learning difficulties of one sort, may in fact be gifted athletes. Having poor literacy skills, or behavioural problems does not necessarily prevent pupils performing well on the sports field. The physical abilities of students do not always match academic ability – an issue to be considered when streaming or setting.

TABLE 2.1 THE FOUR AREAS OF SEN

Cognition and Learning Needs	Behavioural, Emotional and Social Development Needs	Communication and Interaction Needs	Sensory and/ or Physical Needs
Specific learning difficulties (SpLD)	Behavioural, emotional and social difficulties (BESD)	Speech, language and communication needs	Hearing impairment (HI)
Dyslexia			Visual impairment (VI)
Moderate learning difficulties (MLD)	Attention Deficit Disorder (ADD)	Autistic Spectrum Disorder (ASD)	
Severe learning difficulties (SLD)	Attention Deficit Hyperactivity Disorder (ADHD)	Asperger's Syndrome	Multi-sensory impairment (MSI)
Profound and multiple learning difficulties (PMLD)			Physical difficulties (PD)

Provision for staff within the department

In many schools, each department nominates a member of staff to have special responsibility for SEN provision, (with or without remuneration). This can be very effective where there is a system of regular liaison between department SEN representatives and the SENCO in the form of meetings or paper communications or a mixture of both.

The responsibilities of this post may include liaison between the department and the SENCO, attending any liaison meetings and providing feedback via meetings and minutes, attending training, maintaining the departmental SEN information and records, and representing the need of pupils with SEN at departmental level. It is equally vital that this person be aware of and be accessible to, outside support agencies such as occupational health therapists. This post can be seen as a valuable development opportunity for staff. The name of this person should be included in the policy.

How members of the department raise concerns about pupils with SEN can be included in this section. Concerns may be raised at specified departmental meetings before referral to the SENCO. An identified member of the department could make referrals to the SENCO and keep a record of this information.

Reference to working with support staff will include a commitment to planning and communication between staff. There may be information on inviting support staff to meetings, resources and lesson plans.

A reference to the centrally held lists of pupils with SEN and other relevant information will also be included in this section. A note about confidentiality of information should be included.

Example

> The member of staff with responsibility for overseeing the provision of SEN within the department will attend liaison meetings and feed back to other members of the department. He will maintain the department's SEN information file, attend appropriate training and disseminate this to all departmental staff. All information will be treated with confidentiality.

Provision for pupils with SEN

It is the responsibility of all staff to know which pupils have SEN and to identify any pupils having difficulties. Pupils with SEN may be identified by staff within the department in a variety of ways. These may be listed and could include:

- observation in lessons
- assessment of written work

- homework tasks

- end of module tests

- progress checks

- annual examinations

- reports

Setting out how pupils with SEN are grouped within the PE department may include specifying the criteria used and/or the philosophy behind the method of grouping.

Example

> Pupils will be grouped in ways that facilitate their maximum participation in high quality PE and sport experiences. What is important is that each child is given the opportunity to operate within a learning environment that engages them fully and enables them to reach their full potential.

Monitoring arrangements and details of how pupils can move between groups should also be set out. Information collected may include:

- National Curriculum levels

- experience, proficiency in certain areas. For instance, a child might excel at swimming but find team games like basketball and rugby, difficult

- departmental assessments that highlight levels of progress

- advice from pastoral staff

- discussion with staff in the SEN dept

- information provided on IEPs

Special examination arrangements need to be considered not only at Key Stage 3 and 4 but also for internal examinations. How and when these will be discussed should be clarified. Reference to the SENCO and examination arrangements from the examination board should be taken into account. Ensuring that staff in the department understand the current legislation and guidance from central government is important, so a reference to the SEN Code of Practice and the levels of SEN intervention is helpful within the policy. Here is a good place also to put a statement about the school behaviour policy and rewards and sanctions, and how the department will make any necessary adjustments to meet the needs of pupils with SEN.

Example

> It is understood that pupils with SEN may receive additional support if they have a statement of SEN, are at School Action Plus or School Action. The staff in the PE department will aim to support the pupils to achieve their targets as specified on their IEPs and will provide feedback for IEP or statement reviews. Pupils with SEN will be included in the departmental monitoring system used for all pupils. Additional support will be requested as appropriate. Working with the SEN department to produce IEPs relating to a child's physical needs will enable work to be focused more closely around what that child needs to do in order to progress. It will also enable physical activity to contribute to the child's overall development.

Resources and learning materials

The department policy needs to specify what differentiated materials are available, where they are kept and how to find new resources. This section could include a statement about working with support staff to develop resources or access specialist resources as needed, and the use of ICT. Teaching strategies may also be identified if appropriate. Advice on more specialist equipment can be sought as necessary, possibly through LEA support services: contact details may be available from the SENCO, or the department may have direct links. Any specially bought subject text or alternative/appropriate courses can be specified as well as any external assessment and examination courses.

Example

> The department will provide suitably differentiated materials and, where appropriate, specialist resources for pupils with SEN. Additional resources are available for those pupils working below National Curriculum level 3. At Key Stage 4, an alternative course to GCSE is offered at Entry level, and pupils with SEN will be encouraged to follow the route – either vocational or academic – which best fits their preferred style of learning. Support staff will be provided with curriculum information in advance of lessons and will also be involved in lesson planning. A list of resources is available in the department handbook and on the noticeboard.

Staff qualifications and Continuing Professional Development needs

It is important to recognise and record the qualifications and special skills gained by staff within the department. Training can include not only external courses but also in-house INSET and opportunities such as observing other staff, working to produce materials with other staff, and visiting other establishments. Staff may have hidden skills that might enhance the work of the department and the school, for example some staff might be proficient in the use of sign language.

Example

> A record of training undertaken, specialist skills and training required will be kept in the department handbook. Requests for training will be considered in line with the department and school improvement plan.

Monitoring and reviewing the policy

Any policy to be effective needs regular monitoring and review. These can be planned as part of the yearly cycle. The responsibility for the monitoring can rest with the Head of Department, but will have more effect if supported by someone from outside acting as a critical friend. This could be the SENCO or a member of the senior management team in school.

Example

> The Department SEN policy will be monitored by the Head of Department on a planned annual basis, with advice being sought from the SENCO as part of a three yearly review process.

Summary

Creating a departmental SEN policy should be a developmental activity to improve the teaching and learning for all pupils but especially those with special or additional needs. The policy should be a working document that will evolve and change; it is there to challenge current practice and to encourage improvement for both pupils and staff. If PE staff work together to create the policy, they will have ownership of it; it will have true meaning and be effective in clarifying practice.

CHAPTER 3

Different Types of SEN

This chapter is a starting point for information on the special educational needs most frequently occurring in the mainstream secondary school. It describes the main characteristics of each learning difficulty with practical ideas for use in subject areas, and contacts for further information. Some of the tips are based on good secondary practice while others encourage teachers to try new or less familiar approaches.

The special educational needs in this chapter are grouped under the headings used in the SEN Code of Practice (DfES 2001):

- cognition and learning

- behavioural, emotional and social development

- communication and interaction

- sensory and/or physical needs
  (see Table 2.1 in Chapter 2.)

The labels used in this chapter are useful when describing pupils' difficulties, but it is important to remember not to use the label in order to define the pupil. Put the pupil before the difficulty, saying 'the pupil with special educational needs' rather than 'the SEN pupil', 'Pupils with MLD' rather than 'MLDs'.

Remember to take care in using labels when talking with parents, pupils or other professionals. Unless a pupil has a firm diagnosis, and parents and pupil understand the implications of that diagnosis, it is more appropriate to describe the features of the special educational need rather than use the label, for example a teacher might describe a pupil's spelling difficulties but not use the term 'dyslexic'.

The number and profile of pupils with special educational needs will vary from school to school, so it is important to consider the pupil with SEN as an individual within your school and subject environment. The strategies contained in this chapter will help teachers adapt that environment to meet the needs of individual pupils within the subject context. For example, rather than saying, 'He can't do that task', recognise that the task is too difficult, or not appropriate for the pupil, and adapt the work accordingly.

There is a continuum of need within each of the special educational needs listed here. Some pupils will be affected more than others, and show fewer or more of the characteristics described.

The availability and levels of support from professionals within a school (e.g. SENCOs, support teachers, Teaching Assistants) and external professionals (e.g. educational psychologists, Learning Support Service staff, medical staff) will depend on the severity of pupils' SEN. This continuum of need will also impact on the PE teacher's planning and allocation of support staff.

Pupils with other less common special educational needs may be included in some secondary schools, and additional information on these conditions may be found in a variety of sources. These include the school SENCO, LEA support services, educational psychologists and the internet.

Asperger's Syndrome

Asperger's Syndrome is a disorder at the able end of the autistic spectrum. People with Asperger's Syndrome have average to high intelligence but share the same Triad of Impairments. They often want to make friends but do not understand the complex rules of social interaction. They have impaired fine and gross motor skills, with writing being a particular problem. Boys are more likely to be affected – with the ratio being 10:1 boys to girls. Because they appear 'odd' and naïve, these pupils are particularly vulnerable to bullying.

Main characteristics

- **Social interaction**
  Pupils with Asperger's Syndrome want friends but have not developed the strategies necessary for making and sustaining friendships. They find it very difficult to learn social norms and to pick up on social cues. Highly social situations, such as lessons, can cause great anxiety.
- **Social communication**
  Pupils have appropriate spoken language but tend to sound formal and pedantic, using little expression and with an unusual tone of voice. They have difficulty using and understanding non-verbal language, such as facial expression, gesture, body language and eye-contact. They have a literal understanding of language and do not grasp implied meanings.
- **Social imagination**
  Pupils with Asperger's Syndrome need structured environments, and routines they understand and can anticipate. They excel at learning facts and figures, but have difficulty understanding abstract concepts and in generalising information and skills. They often have all-consuming special interests.

How can the PE teacher help?

- Liaise closely with parents, especially over homework.
- Create as calm a classroom environment as possible.
- Allow the pupil to work in the same place for each lesson.
- Set up a work buddy system for your lessons.
- Provide additional visual cues in class.
- Give time for the pupil to process questions and respond.
- Make sure pupils understand what to do.
- Allow alternatives to writing for recording.
- Use visual timetables and task activity lists.
- Prepare for changes to routines well in advance.
- Give written homework instructions and stick them into an exercise book.
- Have your own class rules and apply them consistently.

The National Autistic Society, 393 City Road, London EC1V 1NG
Tel: 0845 070 4004 Helpline (10 a.m. – 4 p.m., Mon–Fri) Tel: 020 7833 2299
Fax: 020 7833 9666; Email: nas@nas.org.uk; Website: http://www.nas.org.uk

Attention Deficit Disorder (with or without hyperactivity) ADD/ADHD

Attention Deficit Hyperactivity Disorder is a term used to describe children who exhibit overactive behaviour and impulsivity and who have difficulty in paying attention. This is caused by a form of brain dysfunction of a genetic nature. ADHD can sometimes be controlled effectively by medication. Children of all levels of ability can have ADHD.

Main characteristics

- has difficulty in following instructions and completing tasks
- easily distracted by noise, movement of others, objects attracting attention
- often doesn't listen when spoken to
- fidgets and becomes restless, can't sit still
- interferes with other pupils' work
- can't stop talking, interrupts others, calls out
- runs about at inappropriate times
- has difficulty in waiting or taking turns
- acts impulsively without thinking about the consequences
- has difficulty in coping in whole-class, competitive situations

How can the PE teacher help?

- Make eye contact and use the pupil's name when speaking to him.
- Keep instructions simple – the one sentence rule.
- Provide clear routines and rules, rehearse them regularly.
- Sit the pupil away from obvious distractions, e.g. windows, the computer.
- In busy situations direct the pupil by name to visual or practical objects.
- Encourage the pupil to repeat back instructions before starting work.
- Tell the pupil when to begin a task.
- Give two choices – avoid the option of the pupil saying 'No': 'Do you want to use your left or right foot to pass the ball?'
- Give advanced warning when something is about to happen. Change or finish with a time, e.g. 'In two minutes I need you (pupil name) to . . .'
- Give specific praise – catch the pupil being good, give attention for positive behaviour.
- Give the pupil responsibilities so that others can see him in a positive light and he develops a positive self-image.
- Know what a particular child's triggers are. For some it could be sugar, whereas for others, sugar has a calming effect. So watch out for the drinks they bring with them to PE lessons and sport sessions. Others could find being in a noisy, packed sports hall difficult.

ADD Information Services, PO Box 340, Edgware, Middlesex HA8 9HL
Tel: 020 8906 9068
ADDNET UK Website: www.btinternet.com/~black.ice/addnet/

Autistic Spectrum Disorders (ASD)

The term 'Autistic Spectrum Disorders' is used for a range of disorders affecting the development of social interaction, social communication and social imagination and flexibility of thought. This is known as the 'Triad of Impairments'. Pupils with ASD cover the full range of ability, and the severity of the impairment varies widely. Some pupils also have learning disabilities or other difficulties. Four times as many boys as girls are diagnosed with an ASD.

Main characteristics

- **Social interaction**
  Pupils with an ASD find it difficult to understand social behaviour and this affects their ability to interact with children and adults. They do not always understand social contexts. They may experience high levels of stress and anxiety in settings that do not meet their needs or when routines are changed. This can lead to inappropriate behaviour.

- **Social communication**
  Understanding and use of non-verbal and verbal communication is impaired. Pupils with an ASD have difficulty understanding the communication of others and in developing effective communication themselves. They have a literal understanding of language. Many are delayed in learning to speak, and some never develop speech at all.

- **Social imagination and flexibility of thought**
  Pupils with an ASD have difficulty in thinking and behaving flexibly which may result in restricted, obsessional, or repetitive activities. They are often more interested in objects than people, and have intense interests in one particular area such as trains or vacuum cleaners. Pupils work best when they have a routine. Unexpected changes in those routines will cause distress. Some pupils with Autistic Spectrum Disorders have a different perception of sounds, sights, smell, touch, and taste, and this can affect their response to these sensations.

How can the PE teacher help?

- Liaise with parents as they will have many useful strategies.

- Provide visual supports in class: objects, pictures, etc.

- Establish a visual timetable of the lesson, so children know what is happening and what will come next. Showing them a towel acts as a sign that it is time to get out of the pool, whereas a ball might mean that it is time to begin the activity.

- Give a symbolic or written timetable for each day.

- Give advance warning of any changes to usual routines.

- Provide either an individual learning area or a work 'buddy'.

- Avoid using too much eye contact as it can cause distress.

- Give individual instructions linked to visual demonstration, using the pupil's name, e.g. 'Paul, stand on the line like John is doing.'

- Allow access to computers.

- Develop social interactions using a buddy system or Circle of Friends.

- Avoid using metaphor, idiom or sarcasm – say what you mean in simple language.

- Use special interests to motivate.

- Allow difficult situations to be rehearsed by means of Social Stories.

BEHAVIOURAL, EMOTIONAL AND SOCIAL DEVELOPMENT NEEDS

This term includes behavioural, emotional, social difficulties and Attention Deficit Disorder with or without hyperactivity. These difficulties can be seen across the whole ability range and have a continuum of severity. Pupils with special educational needs in this category are those who have persistent difficulties despite an effective school behaviour policy and a personal and social curriculum. (See p. 24 for notes on Attention Deficit Disorder.)

Behavioural, emotional and social difficulties (BESD)

Main characteristics

- inattentive, poor concentration and lack of interest in school/school work
- easily frustrated, anxious about changes
- unable to work in groups
- unable to work independently, constantly seeking help
- confrontational – verbally aggressive towards pupils and/or adults
- physically aggressive towards pupils and/or adults
- destroys property – their own/others
- appears withdrawn, distressed, unhappy, sulky, may self-harm
- lacks confidence, acts extremely frightened, lacks self-esteem
- finds it difficult to communicate
- finds it difficult to accept praise

How can the PE teacher help?

- Check the ability level of the pupil and adapt the level of work to this.
- Consider the pupil's strengths and use them.
- Tell the pupil what you expect in advance, as regards work and behaviour.
- Talk to the pupil to find out a bit about them.
- Set a subject target with a reward system, but be aware of general behaviour targets so PE can contribute to overall development.
- Focus your comments on the behaviour not on the pupil and offer an alternative way of behaving when correcting the pupil.
- Avoid situations where the pupil stands out from their peers.
- Use positive language and verbal praise whenever possible.
- Tell the pupil what you want them to do: 'I need you to . . .', 'I want you to . . .', rather than ask. This avoids confrontation and allows the possibility that there is room for negotiation.
- Give the pupil a choice between two options.
- Stick to what you say.
- Involve the pupil in responsibilities to increase self-esteem and confidence.
- Plan a 'time out' system. Ask a colleague for help with this.

- In competitive situations, focus on individual progress rather than outcome in terms of winning, losing – scoring/conceding. Targets relating to individual controllables, such as fitness, can also be used, and 'non-team' activities, such as dance, gymnastics, swimming and athletics, are often ways of engaging children with these difficulties.

SEBDA is the new name for the Association of Workers for Children with Emotional and Behavioural Difficulties.
Website: http://www.awcebd.co.uk

Cerebral Palsy (CP)

Cerebral palsy is a persistent disorder of movement and posture. It is caused by damage or lack of development to part of the brain before or during birth or in early childhood. Problems vary from slight clumsiness to more severe lack of control of movements. Pupils with CP may also have learning difficulties. They may use a wheelchair or other mobility aid.

Main characteristics

There are three main forms of cerebral palsy:

- *spasticity* – disordered control of movement associated with stiffened muscles

- *athetosis* – frequent involuntary movements

- *ataxia* – an unsteady gait with balance difficulties and poor spatial awareness

Pupils may also have communication difficulties. Physical activity is vital for children with these impairments as, without it, their muscles will stiffen and weaken and their condition could degenerate.

How can the PE teacher help?

- Talk to parents, the physiotherapist – and the pupil.

- Physiotherapy targets are usually based around developing strength, stamina and flexibility and can be used as part of whole-class warm-ups.

- Consider the layout of the learning environment.

- Have high academic expectations.

- Use visual supports: objects, pictures, symbols.

- Arrange a work/subject buddy.

- Speak directly to the pupil rather than through a Teaching Assistant.

- Ensure access to appropriate IT equipment for the subject – and that it is used.

Scope, PO Box 833, Milton Keynes, MK12 5NY
Tel: 0808 800 3333 (Freephone helpline) Fax: 01908 321051
Email: cphelpline@scope.org.uk; Website: http://www.scope.org.uk

Down's Syndrome (DS)

Down's Syndrome is the most common identifiable cause of learning disability. This is a genetic condition caused by the presence of an extra chromosome 21. People with DS have varying degrees of learning difficulties ranging from mild to severe. They have a specific learning profile with characteristic strengths and weaknesses. All share certain physical characteristics but will also inherit family traits, in physical features and personality. They may have additional sight, hearing, respiratory and heart problems.

Main characteristics

- delayed motor skills
- takes longer to learn and consolidate new skills
- limited concentration
- difficulties with generalisation, thinking and reasoning
- sequencing difficulties
- stronger visual than aural skills
- better social than academic skills

How can the PE teacher help?

- Sit the pupil in the best position to see and hear.
- Speak directly to the pupil and reinforce with facial expression, pictures and objects.
- Use simple, familiar language in short sentences – stressing one aspect at a time. Abstract instructions such as 'Get in a good defensive position and remember to mark number 5' are likely to result in confusion. Use direct language: 'Keep close to number 5. Stop number 5 from getting the ball. If number 5 gets the ball, try to tackle him and take the ball from him.'
- Check instructions have been understood.
- Give time for the pupil to process information and formulate a response.
- Break lessons up into a series of shorter, varied and achievable tasks.
- Accept other ways of recording: drawings, tape/video recordings, symbols, etc.
- Set differentiated tasks linked to the work of the rest of the class.
- Provide age-appropriate resources and activities.
- Allow working in top sets to give good behaviour models.
- Provide a work buddy.
- Expect unsupported work for part of each lesson.

The Downs Association, 155 Mitcham Road, London SW17 9PG; Tel: 0845 230 0372
Email: info@downs-syndrome.org.uk; Website: http://www.downs-syndrome.org.uk

Fragile X Syndrome

Fragile X Syndrome is caused by a malformation of the X chromosome and is the most common form of inherited learning disability. This intellectual disability varies widely with up to a third having learning problems ranging from moderate to severe. More boys than girls are affected but both may be carriers.

Main characteristics

- delayed and disordered speech and language development
- difficulties with the social use of language
- articulation and/or fluency difficulties
- verbal skills better developed than reasoning skills
- repetitive or obsessive behaviour such as hand-flapping, chewing, etc.
- clumsiness and fine motor co-ordination problems
- attention deficit and hyperactivity
- easily anxious or overwhelmed in busy environments

How can the PE teacher help?

- Liaise with parents.
- Make sure the pupil knows what is to happen in each lesson – provide visual timetables, work schedules or written lists.
- Ensure the pupil sits at the front of the class, in the same seat for all lessons.
- Arrange a work/subject buddy.
- Where possible keep to routines and give prior warning of all changes.
- Make instructions clear and simple.
- Use visual supports: objects, pictures, symbols.
- Allow the pupil to use a computer to record and access information.
- Give lots of praise and positive feedback.

Fragile X Society, Rood End House, 6 Stortford Road, Dunmow, CM6 1DA
Tel: 01424 813147 (Helpline) Tel: 01371 875100 (Office)
Email: info@fragilex.org.uk; Website: http://www.fragilex.org.uk

Moderate learning difficulties (MLD)

The term 'moderate learning difficulties' is used to describe pupils who find it extremely difficult to achieve expected levels of attainment across the curriculum even with a differentiated and flexible approach. These pupils do not find learning easy and can suffer from low self-esteem and sometimes exhibit unacceptable behaviour as a way of avoiding failure.

Main characteristics

- difficulties with reading, writing and comprehension
- unable to understand and retain basic mathematical skills and concepts
- immature social and emotional skills
- limited vocabulary and communication skills
- short attention span
- under-developed co-ordination skills
- lack of logical reasoning
- inability to transfer and apply skills to different situations
- difficulty remembering what has been taught
- difficulty with organising themselves, following a timetable, remembering books and equipment

How can the PE teacher help?

- Check the pupil's strengths, weaknesses and attainment levels.
- Establish a routine within the lesson.
- Allow for repetition of content but provide a variety of short approaches to this content.
- Keep listening tasks short or broken up with activities.
- Provide word lists, writing frames, shorten text.
- Try alternative methods of recording information, e.g. drawings, charts, labelling, diagrams, use of ICT.
- Check previously gained knowledge and build on this.
- Repeat information in different ways.
- Show the child what to do or what the expected outcome is, demonstrate or show examples of completed work.
- Use practical, concrete, visual examples to illustrate explanations.
- Question the pupil to check they have grasped a concept or can follow instructions.
- Make sure the pupil always has something to do.
- Use lots of praise, instant rewards – catch them trying hard.

The MLD Alliance, c/o The Elfrida Society, 34 Islington Park Street, London N1 1PX
Website: www.mldalliance.com/executive.htm

Physical disability (PD)

There is a wide range of physical disabilities, and pupils with PD cover all academic abilities. Some pupils are able to access the curriculum and learn effectively without additional educational provision. They have a disability but do not have a special educational need. For other pupils the impact on their education may be severe, and the school will need to make adjustments to enable them to access the curriculum.

Some pupils with a physical disability have associated medical conditions which may impact on their mobility. These include cerebral palsy, heart disease, spina bifida and hydrocephalus, and muscular dystrophy. Pupils with physical disabilities may also have sensory impairments, neurological problems or learning difficulties. They may use a wheelchair and/or additional mobility aids. Some pupils will be mobile but may have significant fine motor difficulties that require support. Others may need augmentative or alternative communication aids.

Pupils with a physical disability may need to miss lessons to attend physiotherapy or medical appointments. They are also likely to become very tired as they expend greater effort to complete everyday tasks. Schools will need to be flexible and sensitive to individual pupil needs.

How can the PE teacher help?

- Get to know pupils and parents and they will help you make the right adjustments.

- Maintain high expectations.

- Consider the changing room layout.

- Allow extra time for getting changed.

- Allow the pupil to leave lessons a few minutes early to avoid busy corridors and give time to get to the next lesson.

- Speak directly to the pupil rather than through a Teaching Assistant.

- Let pupils make their own decisions.

- Ensure access to appropriate equipment for the lesson.

- Give alternative ways of participating.

- Be sensitive to fatigue, especially at the end of the school day.

Semantic Pragmatic Disorder (SPD)

Semantic Pragmatic Disorder is a communication disorder which falls within the autistic spectrum. 'Semantic' refers to the meanings of words and phrases and 'pragmatic' refers to the use of language in a social context. Pupils with this disorder have difficulties understanding the meaning of what people say and in using language to communicate effectively. Pupils with SPD find it difficult to extract the central meaning – saliency – of situations.

Main characteristics

- delayed language development
- fluent speech but may sound stilted or over-formal
- may repeat phrases out of context from videos or adult conversations
- difficulty understanding abstract concepts
- limited or inappropriate use of eye contact, facial expression or gesture
- motor skills problems

How can the PE teacher help?

- Sit the pupil at the front of the room to avoid distractions.
- Use visual supports: objects, pictures, symbols.
- Pair with a work/subject buddy.
- Create a calm working environment with clear classroom rules.
- Be specific and unambiguous when giving instructions.
- Make sure instructions are understood, especially when using subject-specific vocabulary that can have another meaning in a different context.

AFASIC, 2nd Floor, 50–52 Great Sutton Street, London EC1V 0DJ
Tel: 0845 355 5577 (Helpline 11 a.m. – 2 p.m.) Tel: 020 7490 9410
Fax: 020 7251 2834
Email: info@afasic.org.uk; Website: http://www.afasic.org.uk

Sensory Impairments

Hearing impairment (HI)

The term 'hearing impairment' is a generic term used to describe all hearing loss. The main types of loss are monaural, conductive, sensory and mixed loss. The degree of hearing loss is described as mild, moderate, severe or profound. Some children rely on lip reading, others will use hearing aids, and a small proportion will have British Sign Language (BSL) as their primary means of communication.

How can the PE teacher help?

- Check the degree of loss the pupil has.

- Check the best position in team games – is hearing better on the left or right?

- Check that the pupil can see your face for facial expressions and lip reading.

- Provide a list of vocabulary, context and visual clues especially for new sports/games.

- During class discussion allow one pupil to speak at a time and indicate where the speaker is.

- Allow for the development of a number of non-verbal communication methods between pupils involved in activities.

- Check that any aids are working and if there is any other specialist equipment available.

Royal National Institute for the Deaf (RNID), 19–23 Featherstone Street, London EC1Y 8SL
Tel: 0808 808 0123
British Deaf Association (BDA) 1–3 Worship Street, London EC2A 2AB
British Association of Teachers of the Deaf (BATOD), The Orchard, Leven, North Humberside HU17 5QA
Website: www.batod.org.uk

Visual impairment (VI)

Visual impairment refers to a range of difficulties including those pupils with monocular vision (vision in one eye), those who are partially sighted and those who are blind. Pupils with visual impairment cover the whole ability range and some pupils may have other SEN.

How can the PE teacher help?

- Check the optimum position for the pupil, e.g. for a monocular pupil their good eye should be towards the action.

- Always provide the pupil with his own copy of rules, etc.

- Provide enlarged print copies of written text.

- Check use of ICT (enlarged icons, talking text).

- Do not stand with your back to the window/sun as this creates a silhouette and makes it harder for the pupil to see you.

- Draw the pupil's attention to displays – which they may not notice.

- Make sure the floor is kept free of clutter.

- Tell the pupil if there is a change to the layout of a space.

- Ask if there is any specialist equipment available (enlarged print dictionaries, balls with bells or rice to enable movement to be tracked).

- Manual guidance can assist skill development, so you might, for instance, put your hand together with theirs to demonstrate a tennis forehand or a swimming stroke. Always ensure that another adult (Teaching Assistant, teacher) is present and check school's policy on manual guidance, before using this strategy.

Royal National Institute for the Blind, 105 Judd Street, London WC1H 9NE
Tel: 020 7388 1266   Fax: 020 7388 2034   Website: http://www.rnib.org.uk

Multi-sensory impairment

Pupils with multi-sensory impairment have a combination of visual and hearing difficulties. They may also have other additional disabilities that make their situation complex. A pupil with these difficulties is likely to have a high level of individual support.

How can the PE teacher help?

- The PE teacher will need to liaise with support staff to ascertain the appropriate provision within each subject.

- Consideration will need to be given to alternative means of communication.

- Be prepared to be flexible and to adapt tasks, targets and assessment procedures.

Severe learning difficulties (SLD)

This term covers a wide and varied group of pupils who have significant intellectual or cognitive impairments. Many have communication difficulties and/or sensory impairments in addition to more general cognitive impairments. They may also have difficulties in mobility, co-ordination and perception. Some pupils may use signs and symbols to support their communication and understanding. Their attainments may be within or below level 1 of the National Curriculum, or in the upper P scale range (P4–P8), for much of their school careers.

How can the PE teacher help?

- Liaise with parents.

- Arrange a work/subject buddy.

- Use visual supports: objects, pictures, symbols.

- Learn some signs relevant to the subject.

- Allow the pupil time to process information and formulate responses.

- Set differentiated tasks linked to the work of the rest of the class.

- Set achievable targets for each lesson or module of work.

- Accept different recording methods: drawings, audio or video recordings, photographs, etc.

- Give access to computers where appropriate.

- Give a series of short, varied activities within each lesson. Chaining skills – breaking them down into parts, building up to the whole is a useful technique. So – to throw a ball, look at the target – practise – keep your head still – practise – stand with feet shoulder width apart to keep balance – practise – non-throwing foot forward – practise.

Profound and multiple learning difficulties (PMLD)

Pupils with profound and multiple learning difficulties have complex learning needs. In addition to very severe learning difficulties, pupils have other significant difficulties, such as physical disabilities, sensory impairments or severe medical conditions. Pupils with PMLD require a high level of adult support, both for their learning needs and for their personal care.

They are able to access the curriculum through sensory experiences and stimulation. Some pupils communicate by gesture, eye pointing or symbols, others by very simple language. Their attainments are likely to remain in the early P scale range (P1–P4) throughout their school careers (that is below level 1 of the National Curriculum). The P scales provide small, achievable steps to monitor progress. Some pupils will make no progress or may even regress because of associated medical conditions. For this group, experiences are as important as attainment.

How can the PE teacher help?

- Liaise with parents and Teaching Assistants.

- Identify possible sensory experiences in your lessons.

- Use additional sensory supports: objects, pictures, fragrances, music, movements, food, etc.

- Take photographs to record experiences and responses.

- Set up a buddy rota for the class.

- Identify times when the pupil can work with groups, as using physical activity to engage a child in social interaction can help them immensely.

- Provide choices and experiences alongside non-disabled peers. Children may not be able to jump up and down but they can move certain parts of their body in the same way.

MENCAP, 117–123 Golden Lane, London EC1Y 0RT
Tel: 020 7454 0454 Website: http://www.mencap.org.uk

SPECIFIC LEARNING DIFFICULTIES (SpLD)

The term 'specific learning difficulties' covers dyslexia, dyscalculia and dyspraxia.

Dyslexia

The term 'dyslexia' is used to describe a learning difficulty associated with words and it can affect a pupil's ability to read, write and/or spell. Research has shown that there is no one definitive definition of dyslexia or one identified cause, and it has a wide range of symptoms. Pupils may have difficulties with sequencing, which has implications for PE and sport, may be disorganised and find it hard to remember to bring kit, etc. Pupils may also have trouble with remembering left from right. Although found across a whole range of ability levels, the idea that dyslexia presents as a difficulty between expected outcomes and performance is widely held.

Main characteristics

- The pupil may frequently lose their place while reading, make frequent errors with the high frequency words, have difficulty reading names, and have difficulty blending sounds and segmenting words. Reading requires a great deal of effort and concentration.

- The pupil's written work may seem messy with crossings out, similarly shaped letters may be confused such as b/d/p/q, m/w, n/u, and letters in words may be jumbled, such as tired/tried. Spelling difficulties often persist into adult life and these pupils become reluctant writers.

How can the PE teacher help?

- Be aware of the type of difficulty and the pupil's strengths.

- Allow the use of word processing, spell checkers and computer-aided learning packages.

- Provide word lists and photocopies of rules, etc.

- Consider alternative recording methods, e.g. pictures, plans, flow charts, mind maps.

- Allow extra time for tasks, including assessments and examinations.

- Provide reminders to bring kit, dates of sports fixtures, etc.

- Be aware of potential problems if asking pupils to record results.

The British Dyslexia Association
Tel: 0118 966 8271 Website: www.bda-dyslexia.org.uk
Dyslexia Institute
Tel: 01784 222 300 Website: www.dyslexia-inst.org.uk

Dyscalculia

The term 'dyscalculia' is used to describe a difficulty in mathematics. This might be either a marked discrepancy between the pupil's developmental level and general ability on measures of specific maths ability, or a total inability to abstract or consider concepts and numbers.

Main characteristics

- *In number,* the pupil may have difficulty counting by rote, writing or reading numbers, miss out or reverse numbers, have difficulty with mental maths, and be unable to remember concepts, rules and formulae.

- *In maths based* concepts, the pupil may have difficulty with money, telling the time, with directions, right and left, and with sequencing events or may lose track of turns, e.g. in team games, dance.

How can the PE teacher help?

- Provide photocopies of number/word lists and rules.

- Make use of ICT and teach the use of calculators.

- Plan the setting out of work with it well spaced on the page.

- Allow extra time for tasks, including assessments and examinations.

- Asking children to keep score during a game could prove difficult – consider tallying systems, automatic counters, etc.

Website: www.dyscalculia.co.uk

Dyspraxia

The term 'dyspraxia' is used to describe an immaturity with the way in which the brain processes information, resulting in messages not being properly transmitted.

Main characteristics:

- difficulty in co-ordinating movements, may appear awkward and clumsy
- difficulty with handwriting and drawing, throwing and catching
- difficulty following sequential events, e.g. multiple instructions
- may misinterpret situations, take things literally
- limited social skills resulting in frustration and irritability
- some articulation difficulties

How can the PE teacher help?

- Be sensitive to the pupil's limitations in games and outdoor activities and plan tasks to enable success.
- Ask the pupil questions to check his understanding of instructions/tasks.
- Check seating position to encourage good presentation (both feet resting on the floor, desk at elbow height and ideally with a sloping surface to work on).
- Allow basic facets of skills to be utilised – so sending, receiving from a still or seated position – through to bounce passes and target games, rather than throwing/catching games.

Website: www.dyspraxiafoundation.org.uk

Speech, language and communication difficulties (SLCD)

Pupils with speech, language and communication difficulties have problems understanding what others say and/or making others understand what they say. Their development of speech and language skills may be significantly delayed. Speech and language difficulties are very common in young children but most problems are resolved during the primary years. Problems that persist beyond the transfer to secondary school will be more severe. Any problem affecting speech, language and communication will have a significant effect on a pupil's self-esteem, and personal and social relationships. The development of literacy skills is also likely to be affected. Even where pupils learn to decode, they may not understand what they have read. Sign language gives pupils an additional method of communication. Pupils with speech, language and communication difficulties cover the whole range of academic abilities.

Main characteristics

- **Speech difficulties**
  Pupils who have difficulties with expressive language may experience problems in articulation and the production of speech sounds, or in co-ordinating the muscles that control speech. They may have a stammer or some other form of dysfluency.
- **Language/communication difficulties**
  Pupils with receptive language impairments have difficulty understanding the meaning of what others say. They may use words incorrectly with inappropriate grammatical patterns, have a reduced vocabulary, or find it hard to recall words and express ideas. Some pupils will also have difficulty using and understanding eye-contact, facial expression, gesture and body language.

How can the PE teacher help?

- Talk to parents, speech therapist – and the pupil.
- Learn the most common signs for your subject.
- Use visual supports: objects, pictures, symbols.
- Use the pupil's name when addressing them.
- Give one instruction at a time, using short, simple sentences.
- Give time for the pupil to respond before repeating a question.
- Make sure pupils understand what they have to do before starting a task.
- Pair with a work/subject buddy.
- Give access to a computer or other IT equipment appropriate to the subject.
- Give written homework instructions.

ICAN, 4 Dyer's Buildings, Holborn, London EC1N 2QP
Tel: 0845 225 4071 Email: info@ican.org.uk; Website: http://www.ican.org.uk
AFASIC, 2nd Floor, 50–52 Great Sutton Street, London EC1V 0DJ
Tel: 0845 355 5577 (Helpline) Tel: 020 7490 9410 Fax: 020 7251 2834
Email: info@afasic.org.uk; Website: http://www.afasic.org.uk

Tourette's Syndrome (TS)

Tourette's Syndrome (TS) is a neurological disorder characterised by tics. Tics are involuntary rapid or sudden movements or sounds that are frequently repeated. There is a wide range of severity of the condition, with some people having no need to seek medical help while others have a socially disabling condition. The tics can be suppressed for a short time but will be more noticeable when the pupil is anxious or excited.

Main characteristics

Physical tics

Physical tics range from simple blinking or nodding through more complex movements to more extreme conditions such as echopraxia (imitating actions seen) or copropraxia (repeatedly making obscene gestures).

Vocal tics

Vocal tics may be as simple as throat clearing or coughing but can progress to be as extreme as echolalia (the repetition of what was last heard) or coprolalia (the repetition of obscene words).

TS itself causes no behavioural or educational problems but other, associated disorders, such as Attention Deficit Hyperactivity Disorder (ADHD) or Obsessive Compulsive Disorder (OCD) may be present.

How can the PE teacher help?

- Establish a rapport with the pupil.

- Talk to the parents.

- Agree an 'escape route' signal should the tics become disruptive.

- Allow the pupil to sit at the back of the room to prevent staring, and avoid asking him to 'demonstrate' positions, etc. unless he volunteers.

- Give access to a computer to reduce handwriting.

- Make sure the pupil is not teased or bullied or put in a situation where they may feel vulnerable.

- Be alert for signs of anxiety or depression.

Tourette Syndrome (UK) Association
PO Box 26149, Dunfermline, KY12 7YU
Tel: 0845 458 1252 (Helpline) Tel: 01383 629 600 (Admin)
Fax: 01383 629 609
Email: enquiries@tsa.org.uk; Website: http://www.tsa.org.uk

CHAPTER 4

Creating an Inclusive Environment for PE and Sport

Inclusion values the whole group, but is also concerned with the interests of the individual. The issue is how each person, whatever their ability, can have an experience enabling them to develop to their fullest extent.

From this it follows that an inclusive approach to teaching PE must be child centred – focused on engaging all pupils so that they all enjoy, value and learn from the experience. PE departments need to take account of these matters, even though they have many groups of students and many hundreds of children within them, to consider. While head teachers and their management committees make decisions about the general well-being and development of their students across the whole curriculum, LEAs and other organisations with broader remits have many thousands of children to consider. The remit of national organisations is obviously, even wider. Nonetheless, to be truly inclusive, the individual, the student, the child, must be at the centre and their needs put first!

When developing an inclusive learning environment for PE and sport, we do not have a blank canvas in front of us. In the real world, there are many pre-existing barriers to inclusion, such as attitudes and practices developed over time where the interests of teacher, team and school, LEA, and even government, have been put first. Therefore, the development of inclusive practice is often also about change. To alter delivery, content and style in order to catch the imagination of those groups of youngsters who previously have not been engaged.

It is not impossible to build on existing practices while establishing new values. In many schools a great deal of good inclusive practice is already taking place. Learning from this is about understanding not just how this practice has come about, but showing that it has been effective and that it is transferable to other contexts. It is also about showing why inclusive practice is beneficial – to the school, to the department, to the class and, most importantly – to the individual.

What might an inclusive learning environment for PE and sport look like?

Bearing in mind that many schools were designed and built at a time when few had even heard the word 'inclusion', PE departments need to ask themselves some pretty searching questions about seemingly routine everyday matters if they are to make their learning environment truly inclusive. This is even more crucial if plans to add to, or redesign the school's sporting structure are afoot. For instance:

- Is it physically possible for wheelchair users to be included when their class is timetabled to use a muddy field in the middle of winter?

- Are there two doormats strategically positioned outside the entrance to the changing rooms to stop wheelchairs bringing mud into the school and facing the combined wrath of caretaker and head teacher?

- The school's new Astroturf has just been given a £3,000 facelift. Will the Head of Department allow wheelchairs to buzz around all over it?

- Could sports halls where sun streams in through the windows create blind spots for a child with cerebral palsy, increasing the risk of dangerous collisions?

- Are new sports halls built with smaller adjacent halls so that parallel indoor activities with smaller groups don't have to take place in a corridor or cloakroom?

- Is the presence of thirteen different sets of markings on the floor of the hall likely to assist or confuse the understanding of children with cognitive difficulties or colour blindness?

- Do boards for basketball/netball have to be set, or would adjustable boards fit a wider range of needs?

- Are all pegs in the changing rooms at eye height or are some dropped lower to make it easier for wheelchair users to reach them?

- Are there discreet changing areas for those children who need assistance, so that they do not feel the spotlight is on them?

- Are there toilets big enough for wheelchair users and is there an assistance rail for those who need it?

- Is insisting on white shorts as part of a school uniform any more likely to encourage children with continence needs to want to take part, than making these individuals stand out by allowing them to wear black instead?

- Is there signage to clearly show children how to get from the changing rooms to the gym and the outdoor playing area?

Although physical aspects are important, an inclusive learning environment is also about attitudes and practices. Consider the following hypothetical situation.

School A

Prestige is at stake and the school has traditionally done well in the local U13 cricket league. Parents of these 'elite' youngsters are aware of the school's reputation and expect their team to do well, as does the head teacher. After all, are there not four county players in this year's team? The chair of governors rubs his hands together at the prospect of securing another year's bragging rights – after all, he is a lifetime member of the MCC! Yet during the summer term, time is short and knowledge of the cricketing prowess of the new intake of Year 7s is minimal. The first fixture – ironically against the school's toughest rivals – is a mere four weeks away!

With such motivation determining priorities, might not the PE department be excused if they were to turn the initial weeks of Year 7's PE experience into some sort of 'quick fix' talent identification programme. Rapidly, those with previous experience, 'who look like cricketers', must be picked out and taken off by the two best cricket coaches on the PE staff, while the rest are divided up into large groups and kept occupied. The girls, well as we don't have to have any in the team – they can go off and play rounders. The boy Smith in the wheelchair – give him a pen and paper. He can score!

Success! Later in the year, at the annual awards ceremony, the head teacher proudly displays the under-thirteen trophy to a cacophony of applause from a delighted throng of approving governors and parents.

But is the outcome worth the cost? Sadly, to cricketing purists and competition junkies, the answer may be 'yes'. While elite success and competition has a major part to play in school sport and the knock-on effect in terms of a 'feel-good factor' can be felt throughout the school, the elitist approach also gives out other messages:

- that cricket, indeed sport, is only for the very best

- that PE is about relative performance and only high-level performers are valued

- that talent is about current levels of experience and performance, rather than potential

- that cricket is not for disabled pupils or for girls

Although successful in the eyes of parents, governors and head teacher, School A is engaging only a few children, and it is very likely that these have already developed an interest in the game outside of school. So, in this case, the cost of this particular type of success is the exclusion of the vast majority of children.

School B

With innovation and preparation, performance and inclusion can live side by side. At school 'B', extensive outreach work with feeder primaries has already produced detailed records of the proficiencies, interests and participation levels of all the new Year 7 pupils. A 'gifted and talented' register highlights those who have played at district, county level or above, and a list of those children who are likely because of a specific need, to have difficulty accessing traditional PE and school sport, has also been made.

School B has been entered into the same under-thirteen league as school A but, at the start of the summer term, they have already arranged their PE groups on the basis of the information previously gathered. While more able and experienced children work on advanced skills in the nets with a hard ball and protective equipment, others develop, consolidate and apply more basic skills with soft-ball equipment. Having realised that two members of the year group would be unable to access the mainstream curriculum at the same level and speed as their peers due to physical impairments, the PE department decided to set up a rolling programme of parallel activities for one particular group.

Here, able-bodied children of lower ability and several reluctant participants joined the two wheelchair users, as did a number of youngsters with poor social skills who had previously found it difficult to cope in a more competitive environment. Adapted versions of striking and fielding games allowed balls to be hit from a stationary position and points to be scored through ways other than running. At times, the group played table cricket, a striking game designed specifically for young people with physical or co-ordination impairments. For this group, the aim was as much to engage them in physical activity through providing an enjoyable non-threatening environment, as to develop proficiency. Once engaged, skill development would be quicker long term, as the pupils themselves would be more motivated to learn and improve.

Inclusion was also at the heart of the school's programme of out-of-school-hours cricket. Before each home league game, inter-form, eight-a-side mixed kwik cricket matches took place, with school team players using their knowledge and experience to help out with umpiring and scoring. With eight forms, this meant an additional sixty-four youngsters being given the opportunity to play the game every fortnight. After half-term, coaches from a local club became involved in running the competition, with the last two rounds of matches being played at the club ground in order to encourage some of the new players to join up. Although School 'B' only came third in the inter-school league, by the end of the season, three of the 'kwik cricketers' had made it into the school team. One of the youngsters, who had only picked up a bat for the first time at the beginning of term, showed such natural talent and potential that he was selected for the district under-thirteen squad, the following November.

At the same time a girls' only club was formed taken by a member of the female PE staff who had taken her ECB level one coaching certificate the previous winter. A Year 11 pupil, with some experience of playing cricket herself, provided support. This group was then entered into the local ECB (England and Wales Cricket Board) inter-cricket tournament, from which several girls were chosen to represent the district at the area youth games. After the success of the table cricket sessions, School B's school sport co-ordinator contacted the local authority sports disability officer who found a coach with experience of working with youngsters with physical disability, able to set up an after-school club. Youngsters from nearby primary and secondary schools were also invited to join the sessions, which were paid for out of the county ECB development officer's coaching in schools' budget.

In School 'B' success was measured by more than just elite performance. In giving all their children the opportunity to engage, participate and sustain their involvement, several clear messages were being given:

- PE and sport is for all – whatever your ability.
- Success is about progress and enjoyment as well as winning.

Photo: Simon Harris

- Everyone's success is valued.

- PE and school sport can be the first step into a lifetime of enjoyable participation.

Including the excluded

Often the development of a more inclusive learning environment is about engaging those who, up until now, have either been unable or unwilling to take part or progress in any meaningful way.

Through widespread consultation and a comprehensive audit, the Bexley School Sports Partnership in south-east London discovered that many children with emotional and behavioural difficulties were not accessing the sporting provision offered by their schools. It was realised that, on the whole, these children simply found the activities currently on offer boring! The audit also discovered that throughout the partnership, children with physical disabilities were not getting involved, as they tended to feel that there was nothing on offer for them. Many children with poor social skills tended to choose to do nothing, when the only other options were the sort of competitive team games that they wanted to avoid like the plague!

An Adventure Based Learning (ABL) programme was designed specifically with these groups of children in mind. The Partnership Development Manager for Bexley, Lorraine Everard, stated that:

> Activities needed to offer children with particular difficulties accessing mainstream provision the opportunity to accomplish something on their own terms, whilst also helping meet quite a wide range of special educational needs.

A series of fun, adventure-based tasks allowed children to experience failure as well as success, while also learning to work together. In excess of fifty, easy-to-deliver, equipment-friendly activities were designed to cover a number of key areas, such as initiative, trust, communication, reflection, social responsibility, respect and positive leadership.

In one particularly successful activity, Spider's Web, groups of youngsters designed ways of getting all their members inside a structure which looked a bit like a tent without the canvas. Each child had to get in through a different gap in the structure, which would then be flagged and not available for subsequent use. In this activity, no one could be left out. Everyone had to contribute, asking themselves such things as, 'What order should we go in? Who will need assistance to get through? Which child fits which gap the best?'

Old wooden desktops become stepping stones, in a scenario-based activity in which a large group of students had to get across the swamp of death – or in other words, their school hall or playground! One step in the swamp meant the end for the whole group! The number of stones, each just big enough to get two feet on, was considerably less than the number of people in the group. And don't forget a stone would float only while someone was in contact with it. Lose contact and the stone would sink to the bottom of the swamp forever!

Again, this game required teamwork. Youngsters, many of whom might have had a natural tendency to rush out alone, had to think of their contribution to the whole group rather than just themselves. Co-operation was the cornerstone of another activity in which one child verbally assisted blindfolded partners through a minefield of their own problems. Once the minefield had been successfully negotiated, the issues, represented in the game by coloured cones, were discussed, along with individual and collective solutions.

The scheme was successful in raising participation levels amongst the target groups. Lorraine Everard comments:

> Firstly we made activities accessible, either going to individual schools or transporting children to a central venue ourselves. From here, we designed activities the target groups both wanted and needed and finally we ensured that the right people led the activities. We looked for coaches and leaders with patience and approachability, who could relate to children with specific difficulties and adapt their delivery quickly if things didn't go according to plan.

Inclusive learning environment – how can we tell?

There are, of course, many different ways of developing an inclusive learning environment for PE and sport, all of which can facilitate a high quality of learning and opportunity. Outlined in its publication *High Quality PE and Sport for Young People*, the DfES explained that when such an environment is in place, schools see young people who:

- make PE and sport a central part of their lives in and out of school;

- know and understand what they are trying to achieve and how to go about doing it;

- understand that PE and sport are an important part of an active, healthy lifestyle;

- have the confidence to get involved;

- have the skills and control to get involved;

- take part willingly in a range of group and individual activities;

- think about what they are doing and make appropriate decisions for themselves;

- show a desire to improve and achieve in relation to their own abilities;

- have the stamina, suppleness and strength to keep going;

- enjoy PE, school and community sport.

A guide to help schools evaluate their existing provision and then set about improving and sustaining its quality, the booklet then goes on to examine each outcome in more detail. For instance, pupils who are committed will seldom miss PE or opportunities to take part in sport, will bring kit, and want to take part even if they are ill or injured. They will get changed on time, make themselves available for matches, festivals and performances, encourage others to get involved, and maybe even help adults organise and manage sessions. Similarly, a confident pupil will be willing to demonstrate what they can do, volunteer questions and answers, ask for help when needed and take the initiative to help others. Confidence will allow that youngster to talk positively about what he or she has achieved and be more willing to take part and try new ideas, roles and activities without fear of failure.(See Assessment checklists on CD.)

Above all, if a learning environment is truly inclusive it will enable children to feel comfortable, motivated, empowered, appreciated and able to give of their best. Schools in Cornwall worked with the Global Institute of Student Aspirations (GISA) on a variety of projects designed to raise student aspirations in this very way. Commissioned by the Youth Sport Trust and part funded by the DfES innovation unit, the Cornwall project has enabled three schools: Poltaire School and Community College, Penryn College and Callington Community College to place young people at the heart of their school improvement strategies. Penryn College has been particularly successful in engaging students with special educational needs.

At the time of writing, the number of students with special educational needs at Penryn had increased by 40% over the previous four years. On a roll of 742, 50 pupils are statemented and a further 150 are on the Action and Action Plus programmes. Although there is a wide range of needs, moderate learning difficulties, dyslexia and emotional/behavioural problems are the most common.

GISA has identified eight conditions that affect student aspirations (shown in Figure 4.1 below). The initiative has been designed to help schools find ways to promote these conditions within their given contexts.

At the centre of the work done at Penryn and the other Cornwall schools was the need to listen to students' voices and to find out what they themselves thought about their needs, expectations and their school. An initial survey indicated that, most of all, students wanted to feel a greater sense of belonging, have more leadership opportunities and some fun and excitement in their school lives. In order to do this, a whole-school, whole-curriculum, action plan was put into place.

Firstly it was believed that the aspirations, self-esteem and motivation of pupils with conditions such as ADHD and ASD could be raised by incorporating more opportunities for creativity, curiosity, fun and leadership into lessons. Delivering lessons with more open-ended tasks and allowing pupils to decide on how they wanted to demonstrate learning outcomes was one way of doing this. So, while one group engaged in a movement routine and might wish to show their end product to the rest of the class, another might prefer to put their sequence to music, but to operate at the same time as other groups were working, observed only by the teacher. A third group might simply wish to

Belonging – this entails establishing a sense of community and participation and believing that students are valuable members of that community.

Heroes – research has found that students with high aspirations have a caring adult in their school to whom they feel personally connected, that they can turn to for advice, and can trust. Children need at least one consistent adult in their lives and these adults are not always available at home.

Sense of accomplishment – it is important to recognise and appreciate effort, perseverance, citizenship and the value of learning non-academic subjects.

Fun and excitement – this is about providing an interesting and enjoyable learning environment that makes children excited about learning and enthusiastic about coming to school.

Curiosity and creativity – this is about allowing and encouraging students to question and explore and to keep their inquisitiveness alive.

Spirit of adventure – this is about supporting students who take healthy chances, letting them know it is all right to fail and providing an opportunity for them to understand the consequences of their actions as well as the benefits. Creativity and innovation spring from this.

Leadership and responsibility – this deals with giving every student a voice in the learning environment; letting them know they matter and that they are responsible for their decisions. If students are expected to be independent thinkers they must first be trusted enough to have a voice in their learning.

Confidence to take action – this is about encouraging students to believe in themselves, that they can be successful and make a difference; helping them to be comfortable and assured in their personal and emotional growth.

Figure 4.1 *Conditions affecting students' aspirations*

Source: *Raising Student Aspirations* (2004) Cornwall Learning Forum

report back orally, demonstrating an understanding of the learning that had taken place in their own way.

Alongside this, a contextual approach to learning, enabling students to use their learning styles to participate in lessons more easily, was promoted. A broader variety of activities was offered, with individual sports such as kayaking, sailing, table tennis and judo, not to mention a whole range of outdoor adventurous activities, introduced to supplement the traditional team game approach.

The next step could be for students to become more involved in deciding how their particular style of learning could be incorporated into task design. While some are motivated by competing against their peers, for others the extra pressure inhibits both performance and progress. Similarly, some children work better on their own than in a large group. If the lesson focus during a net/wall module is to improve accuracy when sending, so as to make things more difficult for an opponent, is it not possible to incorporate a variety of activities to cater for different learning styles? Better still, allowing children to develop their own activities, would give further scope for their creative faculties, facilitate independent learning and instil a greater sense of ownership over the outcomes.

The role of the teacher here would be to monitor the nature of the activity to ensure that it enabled every child to focus on the core objectives of the lesson and that activities didn't simply turn into a free-for-all, with fun and enjoyment the *only* outcome.

Penryn is currently working towards developing leadership opportunities which would enable older pupils with conditions such as ADHD to work with, and support, younger pupils with the same condition. It is hoped that this will allow both parties to take ownership of their behaviour, build their self-confidence and self-esteem and improve their performance. Such a mentoring system would help both mentors and mentees identify their own strengths and set goals relating to their Individual Education Plans. The older mentors might also help the other students by demonstrating how best they can work with LSAs to develop their own learning strategies and to track their acquisition of key skills.

To increase the likelihood of success, management at Penryn decided to widen ownership of the initiative by involving the entire community of students and staff. From the outset it was decided to place the responsibility for taking the initiative forward into the hands of those staff who did not already have designated management positions. Currently, 21 members of staff – teachers, Learning Support Assistants, administrative staff, caretaking staff and volunteers – hold some responsibility for implementing the initiative at Penryn College. They make up the Aspirations Team and are led by a designated strategic manager.

(See Case Study on p. 56)

What makes an inclusive PE teacher?

Sue Campbell, Chief Executive of the Youth Sport Trust, speaking at the 2004 Partnership Development Managers' Conference said:

> Everyone has the intention of being inclusive, but are we finding ways of making sure that provision is for all – a life changing experience for every child, no matter what their ability and aspiration? We must do more than simply increase opportunities for those children who already love sport, we must find ways of engaging new children. Not just because we want more to do PE and sport, but because we want the best life chances for all of them and believe that PE and sport can contribute to this.

An inclusive PE teacher would be someone who:

- listens to pupils in order to gauge needs, expectations and wants;
- values the progress and achievement of all, while helping children understand what progress is;
- challenges their own existing practice in order that their delivery might engage a wider range of pupils.

Case study – Elliot, a pupil with achondraplasia

At a school many miles from Cornwall, the aspirations of a student called Elliot have been raised considerably over the last year.

Although Elliot, a youngster with a condition known as achondraplasia (a form of dwarfism) loved sport, there was much his condition prevented him from doing. A fantastic footballer with highly developed skills, Elliot simply couldn't keep up with his peers when involved in a game. Their physical advantages enabled them to run faster, turn more quickly and jump higher. Contact sports, like rugby, were impossible for Elliot, due to spinal weaknesses. He was easily knocked over and it was important to keep his back injury-free.

Like many boys of his age, Elliot was lazy. Finding exercise a chore, he was beginning to put on weight, which caused his back even more problems. As he got older he began to rely more and more on his Learning Support Assistant to help him muddle through PE lessons.

But then it happened. The summer term meant athletics. Long distance running! The fifteen hundred metres! Collective moans! Sudden epidemics of stomach bugs, hay fever and doctor's notes! Although initially reluctant, Elliot decided that he would do the 1500m.

He struggled. But, accompanied by his TA – who carried round a bottle of water to make sure too much fluid wasn't lost (his condition made him prone to sweating) on his way round – Elliot made it. While others had weaselled out of taking part, Elliot had completed the 1500m.

News travels quickly around a school. Other PE staff and teachers from other departments soon found out about his achievements. For the first time, Elliot was being singled out for praise, congratulated on his effort. For a child who compared his own perceived shortcomings to the greater proficiencies of his peers, the sense of accomplishment he felt, was immense.

From this point on, Elliot's attitude to PE changed. Even when he found something difficult, his newfound confidence meant that he was more willing to give it a go. His peers, many of whom had previously 'not wanted to go with the dwarf' in partner or group situations, began to accept him as part of the class. From this he developed a greater sense of belonging, which impacted upon his whole school life. Gradually he became a more confident pupil willing to give of his best in a variety of situations.

Listening to pupils

At Dayncourt School in Nottingham, investigations showed that youngsters with physical disabilities were having difficulties accessing the traditional PE curriculum and were not participating in out-of-school-hours sport. The fact that the school had just been chosen by its LEA, as a through route for disabled pupils and given a £1/4m accessibility upgrade, made the problem more pressing. In order to reverse this trend, the PE department needed to understand the perceptions of the young people themselves. Whilst interviewing fourteen youngsters with physical disabilities, it became apparent that a belief that after-school clubs were only for those who wanted to get better or prepare for school teams, needed to be broken down. Many youngsters lacked the confidence to join up as they felt they simply weren't good enough. However the students interviewed also didn't want to be singled out in their own 'disability group' for fear of it being labelled a 'freak show' by their peers.

From this, the idea of a club designed by and to meet the needs of disabled children, but not populated exclusively by them, was drawn up. Here, children could enjoy activities without pressure, and the option of inviting along able-bodied friends, meant that participants didn't feel that they were being singled out. Table cricket was introduced to this 'Monday Club' via a link with the Nottinghamshire Cricket Board, and both badminton and wheelchair basketball development officers also took advantage of an ideal opportunity to hit their own targets to involve more disabled children in their particular sports. Boccia, a bowls style target game, was also introduced. Since then, Dayncourt's SENCO has asked if several individuals on the register could take part in the club's activities. Currently too timid and shy or lacking the social skills to get involved with any confidence in mainstream sport, it was felt that these children might also benefit from involvement.

The Monday club has also been extended into the community, with local children, experiencing similar difficulties in accessing mainstream sport in their own schools being invited along.

(Naomi's story on page 58 is a good example of how listening to a pupil's concerns can make a big difference.)

> ## Case study – Naomi, a pupil with co-ordination difficulties
>
> Carol Halpin, Inside Out Project Officer with the Nottinghamshire Sports Disability Unit, worked closely with Dayncourt. She describes how listening to an individual helped that student overcome their inhibitions and engage with PE:
>
> 'Whilst visiting a school, I saw one particular girl sitting at the side during what was one of her first PE lessons, as the rest of her Year 7 class were playing netball. I asked Naomi why she was not taking part and she said she wasn't feeling well. Further questioning eventually revealed that at her primary school, Naomi had been hit in the face by a ball, while practising throwing and catching. It transpired that not only did she not want to do PE any more, but that she had got herself so worked up that she had refused to come to school unless her parents wrote her a note excusing her from PE lessons. A few weeks later when I saw the same girl happily taking part in the lesson, I asked the teacher what had happened to change her tune. Previously, Naomi, who has co-ordination difficulties, simply couldn't cope with the sort of fast-paced game of netball, during which she had been struck. She felt that she had neither the technique nor agility to prevent herself being hit again. However, when the class was broken down into smaller ability groups and Naomi was the one chosen from her group to select from a range of balls, not only could she choose a softer ball, one which she felt safe with, but she felt empowered, that it was 'her' game. For the first time, she was taking ownership of her own learning environment. Here she could begin to develop basic skills without fear of injury and progress at her own speed to a point where she is now confident and proficient enough to play games like netball and basketball, with a harder ball. All this had happened simply because the teacher had been willing to listen to the child, find out what was preventing her from joining in and apply a solution to that problem which did not make the child feel she was being singled out.'

Valuing the progress of all

Frank Dick, one of the nation's most highly respected and knowledgeable coaches from the world of sport and business, speaking to delegates from schools all over the country at the Youth Sport Trust's Partnership Development Managers' Conference at Nottingham University in October 2004 said:

> 'Winning should be about being better today, than you were yesterday.'

Children, however, have a natural tendency to compare themselves to the best performer in the group and find a relative perceptual niche for themselves vis-à-vis their peers. How many times have we heard things like, 'Watch out for him – he's really good,' or, 'Ha, ha don't worry about her – she's useless,' only to find that our perception and that of the pupils, of what is good and not so good, really don't match up. Often it is the person who looks good, can do something flash, run the fastest, or hit a ball the hardest or the furthest, who is considered the best by their peers. The more thoughtful, controlled performer and the awkward-looking youngster come right down the bottom on the 'street cred' scale. It is up to teachers and coaches to challenge this 'outcome only' comparative notion of success and to ensure that everyone's progress is registered and the efforts of all are valued.

For children to value progress, they need to understand what it is and see for themselves when it has happened. Everyone comes into a specific situation with a certain level of experience, technical development, natural ability and potential to develop at a certain speed.

Who has done the best? First we have the club standard swimmer. Although she cruises through a series of lessons and wipes the floor with everyone in the races, she is unable to hit her own targets. Through lack of effort she doesn't improve the co-ordination of her leg and arm movements, or significantly eradicate the sideways rolling motion which is affecting her forward momentum, causing her to expend greater levels of energy for less speed. Secondly, there is the child who at the start of the module is unable to swim, but after five weeks, is able to swim ten metres unaided – albeit with a pretty basic technique.

Photo: Simon Harris

If the notion of progress is relative to one's own performance – there is only one real 'winner'. But youngsters may not see this and will need it explained and reinforced through regular discussion during lessons. Progress can be about improving performance, but it can also be about developing a technique or increasing concentration or awareness. For some children it might be about having the confidence to take part or simply enjoying themselves for the first time.

Convincing pupils that learning (in whatever subject area) is about self-improvement is a major challenge. Some pupils never get past the idea that they are 'trying' at school in order to impress family and friends. Some are alienated by the notion of self-improvement from an early age – perversely seeing it as co-operating with a system they hold in low regard. Still other pupils spurn the path of self-improvement through fear of failure. In physical activities, unlike most written tasks, failure is often on public display, so promoting the idea of self-improvement is a key area of engagement for the PE teacher committed to inclusion.

Often youngsters don't progress as quickly as they could during a lesson, but in situations like this it is still possible to turn a negative into a positive. The teacher might, for example, say:

> 'Yes you under-performed in that particular game and you may feel disappointed and think you have let your team or yourself down. But, if you can work out what it is that has caused you to perform below your best and decide what you will try and do next time to put that right, then you have learnt from your mistakes. You now have a greater awareness of and hence more control over your performance. In other words you have progressed during the lesson. You have done well!'

Challenge, innovation and change

Anyone, whatever their profession or vocation, will stagnate if they simply stand still. After Roger Bannister had achieved the impossible and broken the four-minute mile, a whole host of other athletes soon bettered his time. Now four-minute miles are 'ten a penny', with top athletes constantly updating their training methods, just to gain that extra edge over their rivals.

When developing teaching and learning strategies, organising timetables and deciding on priorities, the 'powers that be' are all encouraging innovation. There can be no doubt that the DfES, Ofsted, the Youth Sport Trust and Sport England are all now demanding that the needs of all children be met creatively by schools. At last they are trying to free practitioners from structural straitjackets and allow innovation to flourish.

In some places, however, innovation and creativity is unable to flourish. Where institutional self-interest is the over-riding objective and short-term muddling through the only strategy, inclusive practice is only likely to happen as a result of the presence of an exceptional individual.

Rather than just seeking to increase activity levels in an ad hoc fashion when evaluating their role and performance, School Sports Partnerships must ask themselves a series of questions:

- Have we identified and are we employing the key enabling factors that allow our schools to adopt innovation and take advantage of opportunities for more youngsters to play sport?

- Are systems in place within our schools that allow our primary link teachers and school sport co-ordinators the necessary time to carry out their roles properly? If a primary link teacher (PLT) is expected to perform their role in their own spare time, then they are no more likely to be effective than the school sport co-ordinator who is hardly ever released into the school community as they have 'more pressing' priorities to attend to within their own school.

- Are mechanisms in place to allow us to share good practice from within and outside the Partnership? If one school has organised an alternative break time for their PLTs to enable her fifteen minutes a day to concentrate on widening opportunities and increasing participation levels, or one head teacher has decided to employ a local sports coach as supply cover for his staff, are others aware of this? Are they encouraged to apply similar solutions to their own issues?

- Is the local educational ethos up to date? Are key personnel aware of, or sympathetic towards, the new agenda for PE and school sport? If not, then how can the Partnership pro-actively disseminate the sort of messages necessary to alter attitudes?

- Are all the actors (in schools, LEAs, NGBs, Sports Partnerships) and organisations who play a part in moulding a child's learning environment, singing from the same song sheet? Are their aims in accordance? Do their strategies dovetail?

Unfortunately, implementing solutions to these issues will bring School Sports Partnerships into conflict with the protectors of the status quo: the primary teacher who isn't interested in PE, the Head of PE whose reputation has been built on the success of his rugby and football teams, the SENCO, who after ten years of devoted service, sees her loyalties as first and foremostly to 'her' school, the head teacher to whom SATs or GCSEs are the 'be all and end all' of his *raison d'etre*, the LEA 'bigwig' whose popularity is secured only by the promotion of a 'school-centred' vision of education, the 'non-doing' sports development officer schooled in the days of pen pushing and self-perpetuation and the hockey club chairman who is only interested in talent spotting and inviting the best youngsters to his club.

The list goes on! And under pressure from this army – all of whom will be chanting, 'If it ain't broke don't fix it' to anyone with the inclination to listen, the job of the creative innovator, eager to provide a more inclusive learning environment for their students, becomes more difficult.

So to paraphrase one of the well-known sayings of the President of the European Athletic Coaches Association, Frank Dick: in order to climb their own particular mountains, innovators within PE departments, schools and School Sports Partnerships will have to be resolute and believe in what they are doing. If they do not, there are many people waiting to drag them back down into the valley, should they stumble along the way.

CHAPTER 5

Teaching and Learning

Is it any wonder that so many people have grown up hating PE and sport?

From daisy chains to drill camp

Consider for a moment the idyllic setting of the traditional primary school. It is a lovely summer's afternoon and, for a special treat, Mrs Fussleworth-Potts has decided that the class is to play a game of rounders. After an extended silent reading session has given Felicity and Fleur time to take round the book-club leaflets to the other teachers, the children change in their own good time and take a leisurely stroll over to the field. The office asks Fleur and Felicity if they would mind watering all the plants in the school after they have finished handing out their leaflets.

'It's OK,' beams Mrs Fussleworth-Potts. 'You're only missing PE.'

Soon, Torquil and Tarquin the twins, who had spent the first five minutes of the game making daisy chains and dreaming about their pet bunny, Fluffy, sidle up to their teacher.

'We're cold,' moans Torquil. 'And my tummy hurts.'

Mrs Fussleworth-Potts looks up into the skies. One cloud!

'Well I must admit it is getting a bit parky,' she thinks. 'And I've forgotten my favourite Marks and Spencer's cardy.'

'OK children!' she announces. 'Let's go inside before it starts to rain!'

Sohail, Susan and Stuart, who had all been looking forward to doing PE for the first time in about three weeks, look at each other wryly.

'My dad was right,' says Stuart. 'PE and school sport is rubbish. At least I'm going to football down the road, later tonight.'

Sohail and Susan look sad. Both would love to go to football too, but girls are not allowed to join the club so Susan cannot go, and Sohail's dad is working and so can't get him there.

Stereotypical exaggerations, yes, but imagine the looks on the faces of Fleur, Felicity, Torquil and Tarquin, a year down the line. They have moved on to secondary school and are lined up in the pouring rain for their first cross-country lesson. They are wearing nothing but cotton PE vests and short shorts, and their new PE teachers, Herr Von Sternauss and Ms Spiky, are barking out orders like a couple of prison warders!

'No sore tummies, daisy chains, book-club leaflets and plant watering for you today, mi-lados!'

Two serious questions can be posed from all of this:

1. What are we trying to achieve from our teaching of PE and sport?

2. Is the sudden transition from the 'optional fun' of primary PE to 'compulsory learning' at secondary school, responsible for the disengagement and subsequent long-term exclusion of many children from involvement?

Inclusion or performance?

Contrary to popular belief, there does not have to be a conflict between the two. It is possible to deliver PE and sport in a way which leads to elite success in terms of individual and team performance, while still meeting the needs and facilitating the development of all students.

However, existing practice – in terms of activities offered and methods of delivery – often excludes by its very nature. In many ways, a very traditional 1960's, middle-class, public school curriculum in still in place. Lacking variety, it lends itself to a certain 'skills and drills', 'teams and fixtures' type of teaching, which can limit practitioners to thinking more in terms of the needs of a sport rather than an individual. We often ask ourselves what a child needs to do to be able to play rugby to a certain level, or what a group needs to do to be ready for their hockey match in three weeks' time. How often do we think about what a pupil or group need in order to engage in physical activity, or what physical activity can contribute to individual development? Traditional approaches may enable school teams to be successful and enable some pupils (usually those already interested) to do well at GCSE PE. But unless we adapt both delivery and organisation to meet a range of needs and interests, how will we ever widen participation rates, engage a wider range of pupils, and help them realise their potential?

Learning styles

Staff at Redbridge Upper School in Southampton have proved that there is more than one way to teach PE. Teaching strategies based on preferred learning styles will not only motivate more children to give of their best, but will also raise standards, not to mention widen and sustain participation rates.

Case study: Redbridge

Research identified four key 'route ways' into which children were streamed:

- competition and co-operation
- physical activity
- challenge
- movement and aesthetics

Although the same Programmes of Study have been delivered to all groups, teaching strategies and activities are designed to meet the needs of the particular learning style. An outline of each route, giving key factors against which children can be assessed, is given below.

Pupils who choose the **competition and co-operation** strand will feel that they learn best when:

- working in competitive games and games-related activities;
- applying skills and principles learned in a game situation;
- being encouraged to meet the demands of a variety of game situations – including working towards targets and against opponents;
- developing the concepts of teamwork and fair play in a variety of roles;
- becoming involved in games-related fitness.

An introduction to an invasion games unit for pupils in this strand would be to play a typical 4 v 4 game, where the aim is to beat not only your opponents' score but improve your own score, after each outing. Skill development here is motivated by success, measured in terms of relative, but also personal outcome.

Pupils who choose the **physical activity** strand will feel they learn best when:

- participating in physical activity, not necessarily sport;
- finding out about their own well-being and how to develop this out of school;
- applying this knowledge to a range of physical activities;
- addressing all aspects of fitness – mental, social, physical, psychological;
- warming up, cooling down and learning how to plan personal exercise programmes.

Playing the above as a 2 v 2 game would result in each individual being more actively involved for the whole game. It is the effect of the game on themselves, rather than its outcome, which will motivate the participants to give of their best. At regular time outs, children can check their heart rate, and building their own programme of stretching and resting into the game will increase their awareness. Skill development here is motivated by the relationship between performance and movement, e.g. moving into space to receive the ball, moving into position to intercept a pass made by an opponent. What happens if you stand still when defending and attacking?

Pupils who choose the **challenge** strand will feel they learn best when:

- demonstrating major personal or team success;

- being involved in problem-solving activities – both physical and psychological challenges;

- working towards targets set for and with them;

- developing teamwork and co-operative skills;

- developing organisational, officiating skills, in particular alongside physical ones;

- learning new activities and new skills facing personal challenges and setting short-term targets and long-term goals.

Introduce the same 4 v 4 activity as a series of challenges, giving them scope to select and combine a variety of invasion principles and styles:

- How can we score as many points as possible?

- How can we prevent the other team from scoring?

- How can I contribute to and improve my own and my team's performance?

Pupils who choose the **movement and aesthetics** strand will feel that they learn best when:

- focusing on qualities associated with improving individual performance;

- becoming involved in activity that concerns personal qualities (mental as well as physical) associated with aesthetic performance;

- developing the skills to evaluate and improve performance in a variety of activities;

- working in individual activities;

- showing a penchant for knowledge and skills associated with awareness and expression.

Alter the game to 5 v 5, marking off the playing area into zones within which players have to stay, to give each individual a more clearly defined role in the game. Each player can then consider the mental and physical skills they need to use in order to improve their own performance in that particular role. Working with their opposite number in the other team, they can then start to develop those skills, observing each other and concentrating on the key technical points, relevant to their particular role.

Targeting activity

At the time of writing, Public Service Agreement targets are looming. Within School Sports Partnerships 75 per cent of pupils must be receiving at least two hours of high quality PE and sport weekly by 2006, rising to 85 per cent by 2008, beyond which these figures must be at the very least, sustained. If PE and sport is to retain its current profile, let alone increase its importance within the grander scheme of things, schools simply have to deliver to a greater number of pupils. *The Impact of School Sports Partnerships*, the results of the first DfES's PE School Sport and Club Links (PESSCL) survey, conducted by TNS Social Research and commissioned by the DfES was released in April 2004. It showed that in order to widen engagement, several groups needed targeting:

- Key Stage 1 pupils

- girls

- students with an ethnic heritage

- students with special educational needs

- Key Stage 4 students

From this, it follows that when designing schedules, activities and considering methods of delivery for pupils with special educational needs, the requirements of the target group must drive any changes introduced. There are three questions we must ask in order to ensure a positive learning experience:

1. Who is being targeted?

In order to answer this question it is necessary to find out who is not participating in current activities and why, and to establish the quality of experience of those involved. Informal chats, pupil questionnaires, parents' evenings and conversations with staff in other departments and with form tutors, and proactive outreach while children are still in primary school are all useful ways of gathering information.

One special school used pictorial diagrams and Makaton symbols (see www.makaton.org) to enable children to develop an activity diary. Here they included time, location, who they were with, whether they had chosen to be there or not, what they were doing, and whether they had enjoyed it or not. Pupils were also issued with a camera to take pictures as supporting evidence. Completed on different days of the week over a period of time, the diaries were compared to establish individual patterns and trends relating to children's preferences.

2. What do we want our target group to achieve?

First Steps, a guide to developing quality out-of-school-hours learning PE and sport opportunities for young disabled people and those with special educational needs, quotes a special school teacher as saying:

'Having a purpose and direction helps you to remain focused on the goal and move towards it. For some young people, small steps can be as significant as large ones are for others.'

Depending on the individual, outcomes, based on criteria outlined in *First Steps* could be:

- *Personal* – relating to perceptions of self and environment. Building confidence through involvement could be about getting to know a new teacher or coach, or simply realising that it is possible to take part, have fun and feel safe all at the same time.

- *Educational* – relating to increased proficiency, greater knowledge or self-awareness. Tackling new skills in a club setting can put children who have difficulty accessing mainstream PE and sport as quickly as their peers (because of a special educational need) on a more equal footing with their classmates during curriculum time.

- *Practical* – enabling specific social barriers to be overcome. A club might link isolated disabled pupils in mainstream schools with a special school, or provide a chance for special school pupils to engage with non-disabled peers and build friendships out of school, while at the same time increasing disability awareness.

- *Life-enhancing skills* – Young disabled children may have issues around communication and a smaller learning environment may be suitable to encourage interaction through PE and sport.

Involving children in discussions about purpose, strategy and outcomes will enable them to take ownership of activities, contribute to their design and direct subsequent teaching and learning. However abstract words like 'purpose', 'strategy' and 'outcome' might appear, questions about them can always be pitched in a manner which involves pupils with SEN.

3. What appealing and engaging activities can we design to support the target group in achieving their learning objectives?

In a mixed-ability setting, choosing from a full range of strategies and applying them to the needs of the group and the individuals within it, is the best way to ensure all children have a positive experience. Initially, this could be a case of trial and error, but increased knowledge of and familiarity with the group, will allow key strategies to emerge. The Inclusion Spectrum, initially developed by Joseph Winnick, Professor of Physical Education at Brockport College in the USA, in his book, *Adapted PE and Sport*, and first published in 1982, was adapted in 1997 by a collaboration between the Youth Sport Trust, Liverpool Community College and the British Paralympic Association to meet the needs of children in the UK. It consists of five approaches to the delivery of PE and sport, each seeking to engage both disabled and non-disabled pupils.

Open activities, based on what the whole group can do, immediately get the whole group involved and are an important way of establishing a feeling of group inclusion. During these, everyone can achieve a degree of success. In *modified activities* everyone has the same learning focus but accesses it in different ways, with changes to either the rules, area played in or equipment used. For instance, during a net/wall games session, a young disabled person may be practising their skills using a balloon and a lightweight racket alongside others using more traditional equipment. Although similar conceptually, *parallel activities* see everyone playing the same game, but different groups playing in different ways and at different levels. For instance, tee ball may be played alongside rounders, with the teacher or coach focusing on the same rules, skills or tactics. While *separate activities* give pupils the option of working on a totally different activity from the rest of the group, *disability sports* can be included as part of the curriculum for everyone.

From traditional sport to inclusive PE

For a mixed-ability class of Year 9 pupils, an eleven-a-side game of football is not inclusive. Many pupils will be excluded as they lack sufficient technical or social skills to perform adequately against their peers in a competitive situation. Mobility issues could also cause difficulties for some. The harsh reality of the situation is that, however much we might want them to play 'proper sport', when 22 youngsters are playing a single game, at any one moment, most of them are not actively involved. Even the better players would make little progress in this situation, as they could dominate without really extending themselves.

Dividing the class up into small groups and several games would be the first step on the road to inclusion. With several games taking place simultaneously, each child would get more touches of the ball and a more constant involvement in the game. With a range of abilities, activities can be modified to meet needs, So while the top group played their game with a smaller ball or even used two balls within their match to extend their skills and awareness, less able children might be given a slightly larger area to play in or be put up against a team of fewer members. Tasks themselves can also be different – so as the more able group concentrated on working out for themselves whether zonal or 'man to man' marking systems worked best when defending, a less able group might concern themselves with a more structured introduction to one or the other.

Moving away from a sport-centred towards a child-centred approach enables teaching to become more inclusive. Remembering that the real module focus is invasion games and not football, rules can be adapted to allow a wheelchair user, unable to tackle in the conventional way, to either use their hands or a fishing style net to intercept a ball, when defending. Thinking in terms of generics rather than specific sports enables separate, but related activities to take place. Is there any reason why during the six-week 'football' block, one group per week could not adapt their activity so that the invasion game is played with hand-held sending and receiving skills?

With mixed-ability groups, zoning can be a useful strategy. In the above game, the pitch can be divided into three areas within which certain players must stay during any one passage of play. While in the end zones, pupils have the ball at their feet and pass, tackle and move in the conventional way, in the middle zone, children tackle with the net, while sending and receiving the ball with their hands. This means that students using wheelchairs can use their abilities to engage in the game and progress, without the possibility of collisions or other children being tripped by nets. Able-bodied pupils would switch between zones, taking up each role in turn.

Zone hockey utilises similar strategies in order to integrate ambulant and mobility-impaired players into the same game. With three to seven players, the pitch is divided into three longitudinal zones, with goal areas at each end and a goal, two metres across and one metre high. The central zone represents 50 per cent of the playing area and the two wing zones, 25 per cent each. Players matched by ability must stay within their own zone at all times, and safety dictates no physical contact and that sticks, even light plastic ones, must not be lifted above waist height. TOP Sportsability contains a number of similar games specifically designed to include young disabled people in both the curriculum and out-of-school-hours sport.

Just like its more traditional counterpart, Zone hockey enables pupils to access all four National Curriculum strands for PE. While acquiring and developing skills, children learn to control the ball, shoot from a still position (seated or standing) or on the move, as well as pass to a target or partner. Recognising and using the zones increases spatial awareness, while goalkeeping skills such as moving laterally, blocking and ball distribution are also necessary in this game. To select and apply skills and tactics, children decide whether to control the ball before making a pass or shot, stroke the ball first time, select the correct weight of pass, and play a pass into the path of a moving team mate. When goalkeeping, decisions about such things as whether to narrow the angle by moving towards an opponent or stay on the line, making oneself big, need to be made. In the same way as they would if engaged in a mini hockey session, criteria around how to improve performance might be: to decide when to pass or when to shoot or when to communicate with team mates to keep possession. Getting children to think about how exercise affects them during the game as well as to realise that a physical warm-up might not be appropriate for all participants and might need to be replaced by a mental 'get-ready' for some, would enhance their understanding of health and fitness.

Mixed-ability or group teaching requires the teacher to assume a role and perspective different from the traditional ones. Rather than taking centre stage as the fount of all knowledge, the teacher becomes more of a guide or enabler, making deliberate, well-timed and critical interventions to impart crucial information and give quality feedback. Instead of barking out instructions from the front or centre of the class, the inclusive PE teacher spends more of his/her time talking with individuals or small groups. Sometimes this might involve verbal praise or encouragement; at other times, it could be making one pupil aware that his or her team is reliant on the performance of all its members, not just the best player. Some pupils respond better to questions from which they can work out for themselves what they need to do. Why were you unable to hold that position for more than a few seconds? On the other hand, others will feel challenged by this tactic and perceive it as an attack on their efforts. These children might be engaged more effectively by a re-demonstration of a similar mistake, where it is not they who have done wrong in the eyes of their peers. Some will need to visualise a technique, whereas others will need to gain a greater understanding of what the technique is about or its short-term or long-term purpose, in order to progress.

Two children are both having trouble connecting cleanly with the ball because they are playing their shot too early. A repeat demonstration of the shot to the first, or showing to the second exactly where the ball must get to before they hit, could facilitate greater progress for that particular individual. It may well be that a third child, in their eagerness not to make a mistake, is moving into position the second that they see the ball released from the sender's racket or hand. A critical intervention for this youngster would be to help them to relax, back their own judgement on when to move and not to fret about making a mistake.

When utilising this teaching style, one of the most important functions of the teacher is to help pupils see for themselves what it is they are aiming for and to raise pupil awareness of the process by which they might effectively pursue their objectives. When teaching to core tasks, in the manner suggested by the QCA, the learning process becomes even more vital as students build up knowledge over a number of sessions. However, many children will not naturally think in a logical way and will need support with this. Questions such as, 'What do you need to do next?' or, 'How can you achieve that?' will get them to think about their current performance and what might need altering or adapting in order to progress. Others such as 'What is preventing you from achieving that goal?' or 'What happens if you are distracted by the group next to you?' will help children think about how to minimise the effect of hindrances. Finally, asking children to consider how they know whether they have done well will enable them to realise that making progress is more than about just winning or being the best in the class.

All of these types of questions are related to process rather than content, helping children to develop their own learning strategies. A more regimented approach would undoubtedly give the teacher more control over outcomes, e.g. 'This is how you hold the racket and this is how you hit the ball. I'm going to watch each of you in turn to make sure you do it properly.' Such a style might also appear to produce more rapid initial progress, and mean that the teacher could conclude, 'Well at the end of the lesson nearly everyone could hit the ball like I showed them, so it must have been a good lesson!'

Whereas some children may need a more structured 'watch-do' type experience at times, do we really want an army of robotic clones who can only perform in one way under close supervision? Imparting vital information either through demonstration, explanation or questioning, before allowing each individual to go away and interpret that information in their own way, will in the long term reap greater dividends. In this way, youngsters will be able to build upon and apply the new knowledge or technique on top of what they can already do, rather than having to start from scratch every time. Reliant on themselves and their team mates, they will also become more independent learners and performers, eventually able to out-think and out-play those who have been spoon-fed with abstract knowledge. The latter – their learning having been linked to the context which they were in – will find it very difficult to adapt their skills and knowledge to the requirements of another. Especially if the teacher is not there!

Success for All – an inclusive approach to PE and school sport

A resource, relevant to both primary and secondary children, Success for All uses the inclusion spectrum as a starting point for a number of interactive case studies and lesson ideas. Produced by the DfES in conjunction with the English Federation of Disability Sport, the QCA, the Youth Sport Trust and Inclusion, the resource also offers useful tips for teaching children with physical disabilities within mainstream classes. Indicative of its general nature is its approach to dance.

Dance

An interactive case study features a group of pupils from a mainstream and a special school working together on a joint dance project. Here they explore ways to choreograph a dance sequence, focus their awareness of body parts, and develop an understanding of shape and levels. While involved, all the pupils express themselves and use their imagination to appreciate dance. Any part of the body can be utilised during dance and while power-chair users might need to use joysticks or switches, their movement is equally valid. Children with minimal movement can use their head, shoulders, mouth and face to good effect and because of this, the creativity of the mainstream pupils to utilise facial expression while dancing was improved.

Split up into four sections – an activity overview, working together, inclusive teaching and improvement/performance – the lesson is supplemented by visual illustrations and video interviews with the teacher, head teacher, pupils and a parent of one of the disabled children. More detailed support on delivering dance to children with special educational needs is also given in a supporting document, encouraging teachers to:

- Use a range of sounds, such as percussion, pop music, music from other cultures.

- Use a variety of apparatus, such as balloons, ribbons, material, bubbles, scarves or hoops.

- Develop pupils as choreographers. Give them a sound structure and let them develop the detail.

- Adapt movement concentrating on what a child can do rather than what they can't, so if they can't use one side of the body, encourage them to use the other or facilitate one side, or to use hands instead of feet.

- Aim for a mood rather than a complicated step pattern with some pupils.

- Use a pupil's aid as a prop or a focus.

- Move from concrete concepts to more abstract ones.

- Use repetitive patterns.

- Use visual and sound cues.

- Use particular pupils as visual cues for pupils to follow, move towards, finish behind or in front of. A pupil with learning difficulties might be set a task to mirror a non-disabled pupil's movement (or vice-versa in a buddy system).

- Encourage some pupils to undertake certain movements through colour-coded prompts, e.g. red – stop, green – go, blue – move to the right.

The resource goes on to explain how pupils with learning disabilities may not be aware of abstract concepts such as elevate, spiral or hover, until they have experienced them first hand. Teachers can help some pupils to discover the meanings of words by demonstrating an appropriate movement. Some pupils may need to hold or feel objects, such as using a fan to recreate walking against the wind, or see a picture or a video of an animal before trying to copy its movements. Teachers can encourage pupils to increase their movement vocabulary by asking them to try to name the movements they make. With pupils who have a visual impairment (VI), other strategies can be adopted:

- Alternatives to visual imagery can be found, for example using tactile imagery such as 'the hot sun', 'a cool, gurgling river', or giving physical clues, such as 'a pointed, church spire'.

- Manual tracking can be incorporated. For example, a pupil with a VI can follow the path of a movement by placing their hand on the back of a sighted partner's hand. This can then be repeated with sighted pupils tracking their visually impaired partner's movement.

For pupils with a short attention span, different combinations of tactile, verbal, musical and visual stimuli can help them to focus on an activity. Pupils who have a hearing impairment can be included more fully in dance activities by appreciating the way that sound is created and used in the dance. Live instruments are easier for pupils to appreciate than recorded sound, as they can feel the resonance of a wind instrument, or they can touch a drum while it is played in different ways. Further ideas for including pupils with disabilities in Dance can be found in the Youth Sport Trust (YST) *TOP Dance* cards. Ideas for including pupils with profound and multiple disabilities in movement and dance activities (including rebound therapy can be found in the 'Fire' section of the YST/English Federation of Disability Sport *Elements* cards.

Much can be learnt from experienced and gifted teachers working in environments where both inclusion and PE and sport are high profile. However, transferring the type of teaching and learning strategies featured so far in this chapter can be constrained by traditional curriculum and school organisation. Innovation here can facilitate the sort of inclusive teaching shown on the Success for All CD-Rom.

At Knottingley High School in Wakefield, the whole school day has been re-organised in order to do just this. PE has been taken out of mainstream curriculum time and is now taught in a two-hour block at the end of a shorter school day. Because of this, each year group gets one two-and-a-half-hour slot per week, divided up into mainstream curriculum time and an hourly enrichment session. Technically an out-of-school-hours learning experience, the enrichment session is compulsory, but students get to choose which activity they do from a very long and varied list. Activities such as table tennis, judo, badminton, fencing and gymnastics are offered alongside the more traditional team games, to cater for a wider range of tastes.

Organising the curriculum in this way has allowed the PE department to arrange groups according to physical ability, rather than simply deal with a class which may have similar academic standards, but could contain a very wide range of physical needs. At the time of writing, the current Year 7 support group has within it, children with a range of special educational needs. However, alongside a child with ADHD, two dyspraxic students and several with visual and hearing impairments, there are also several youngsters who have either low physical ability or lack of experience, resulting from opting out at primary school.

During their gymnastics module, the emphasis for the support group was on group work. With less demanding physical performance outcomes required of them, the pupils were given a very structured set of processes, with an open-ended outcome which rewarded effort as much as proficiency. The teaching approach was simply – explain it, view it, do it! Firstly, a concept such as rotation would be introduced in its simplest form: What is rotation? What areas of the body might be used? Next, demonstrations, often using video, were given to enable pupils to link the abstract to the real. Lastly, pupils were asked to explore their own variations, giving them the chance to use their creativity and develop greater independence. Dave Tromans, the Director of Sport at the school, explained: 'By personalising their educational experience in this way, we

Case study – Daniel, a pupil with EBD

Daniel – a very small, not particularly robust boy with numerous emotional and behavioural issues – arrived at Knottingley High with a history of non-participation at primary school. He had all the usual strategies – feigning illness, forgetting kit, doing as little as possible when involved and hoping no one would notice – 'off to a tee'.

Fortunately the school's organisation of PE meant that both the time of PE staff and the school's facilities were available to local primary schools during the mornings and so Daniel's lack of engagement with PE and sport did not come as a surprise to his new teachers. After a single term, not only had Daniel's baseline PE assessment gone from a 2C to a 3B, but he had secured 100 per cent participation.

As part of a 'weak and vulnerable group', Daniel had been given the opportunity to take part in off-site, outdoor, adventurous activities. Benefiting from team building, activities based around social interaction enabled Daniel to develop the confidence and capacity to engage with the mainstream curriculum.

Early on in his first term, the first inter-house competition – cross-country – was organised during one Year 7 enrichment session. An inclusive, compulsory activity where everybody took part and everybody scored points, was preferred to the sort of selection based on 'turn up if you want to take part' approach. For Daniel – who would have never been picked or thought about coming along off his own back – this was the start of his engagement with PE. He loved the competition. Being part of a team working towards a group goal, but with control over his own individual contribution, gave him a greater sense of belonging. Since then, Daniel has been to every after-school cross-country club, and has even represented the school.

He may never be a superstar runner or win these races, but he has progressed dramatically since he began and the effect on his confidence and self-esteem has been marked. Without the curricular innovation his school provided, an inter-house event of this type would have been impossible to organise and Daniel might never have got involved.

feel that all children can experience success, progress and enjoyment at their own level.'

Participation in PE and sport can also have a major effect on pupil behaviour. As one of a number of schools involved in the Living For Sport Programme, Eltham Green Sports College in Greenwich discovered how physical activity can make a positive difference to the motivation and enthusiasm of youngsters at risk of disengaging from the learning process. Living for Sport, funded by Sky TV and organised by the Youth Sport Trust, was launched nationally after a successful pilot in 2002. The scheme provides resources, funding and training for teachers. Richard Little, Director of Sport at Eltham Green School, commented:

> 'Since the project began in January 2003 I have noticed positive changes, both in the attitude of individuals in the target groups and the atmosphere of the school as a whole. Initially, we needed to help these youngsters develop a greater sense of belonging. This meant challenging departmental practice and delivering a PE curriculum which could make a real contribution to a group whose difficulties with a traditional diet of teaching and academia, were causing them to opt out of school life altogether.'

Rather than focusing on skills and drills, PE activities have been used to develop confidence and self-esteem, helping create a learning environment in which vulnerable pupils feel secure enough to give of their best. Expressing themselves without fear of ridicule, students were asked to post on sports hall whiteboards, the names of anyone they noticed acting responsibly or being helpful during PE lessons. Then, in plenary sessions, youngsters – whose natural inclination to self-centredness and negativity towards the efforts of others had previously hindered their progress – complimented each other, explaining why someone deserved a particular accolade. As well as raising awareness of the needs of others, such an approach also encouraged more careful observation, helping students evaluate and improve their performance more effectively in subsequent PE lessons.

Since the initial pilot phase of the project came to an end in September 2003, Eltham Green have extended their Living For Sport programme to benefit a wider range of students. In partnership with the London Leisure College, a Sport and Progression City and Guilds Course has been developed. At the college – situated within the stadium of premiership football club, Charlton Athletic – a targeted Year 10 group now take lessons in customer care, first aid and the junior sports leader's award. As well as giving them the chance to develop the key interpersonal skills they currently lack in an essentially adult environment, these pupils, previously at risk of permanent exclusion, now have a real incentive to come to school. In the hands of the learning support department, knowledge gained during the pilot phase of the programme is also being applied to the rest of the curriculum. A new group of potentially disaffected Year 9 students are currently completing Living For Sport Planners in order to raise their own aspirations and work out how they might develop a greater sense of belonging to the school community.

CHAPTER 6

Monitoring and Assessment

She tries hard and always has a smile on her face, but due to her lack of mobility Sunita is unable to take part in most team games, so we are unable to give an accurate assessment of what she can do. Although she is 'sport mad' we recommend that she prioritises academic study over PE, when choosing her GCSE options, next year. (End-of-year school report)

Two months after this end-of-year report, Sunita took part in a swimathon at her club, to raise money for a local charity. She swam two miles. Her school didn't have a pool – so they didn't do swimming!

Assessment should be about discovering what a pupil can do, not highlighting what they cannot. It is about helping children understand what has enabled them to get to a certain point and identifying strategies by which they can progress further or, if required, in alternative directions.

Assessment should be:

- child centred

- concerned with process as well as outcome

- concerned with more than just performance and skills (e.g. feelings and attitude)

- part of an ongoing dialogue between both teacher and student and pupils and their peers, which informs future learning – and future teaching

Formative assessment

Although many School Sport Partnerships are working to address the problem, it is a common complaint that primary school PE assessment procedures do not always provide sufficient detail from which to work. Yet, throwing a group of new Year 7s into a rigorous performance-based assessment programme is unlikely to give an accurate picture of what all can do. For any number of personal, social or emotional reasons, many youngsters may simply not be able to do their best in their first few weeks at a new school. Several schools have overcome this problem by designing a transition curriculum for PE. As well as providing initial formative assessment, these innovations tend to concentrate on engaging pupils, sharing information, establishing departmental expectations and introducing school ethos. If a performance-based assessment is required at this stage, it might prove more fruitful for the primary feeders to do it.

As far as possible, pupils are taught PE in their primary school groupings for their first four months at Hailsham Community College in East Sussex. Keeping the new Year 7 intake with friends from primary school means that they are able to get used to the rules, expectations and ethos of the Sports College in a less intimidating environment. Not having to waste time dealing with relationship issues because they already know each other, pupils can more readily concentrate on learning.

Each group is introduced to a range of 'basic skills' modules, which covers the sorts of fundamental movements and techniques on which they can build throughout their school lives. During the course of this initial assessment period, each pupil is given a logbook outlining the PE programme and explaining what he or she could expect to learn in each module. At the end, the pupils reflect on the skills they have learned, consider their attitude towards PE and set themselves targets for future learning in that activity.

From here, children are grouped according to ability, with a small nurture group set up for those youngsters who need specific support to access the curriculum.

Benefiting children with emotional and behavioural difficulties, nurture groups are seen to be an effective way of preventing further disaffection, allowing re-engagement with a subject and increasing personalised learning. In a nurture group, adults act as role models, demonstrating appropriate behaviours. A small group of ten to twelve pupils at most enables a great deal of individual support and attention to be given. Although the National Curriculum can be followed, there is an emphasis on the development of social and communication skills as well as a therapeutic approach where, for instance, music might be used within a lesson to generate a calm atmosphere. While positive behaviour is praised, negative is, as far as possible, ignored. Even the simplest of tasks will be structured into stages, focusing on the development of self control – although, initially, the teacher will limit choice and establish routines in order to show children ways in which they can regulate their own behaviour.

Anna Robinson, the Director of Sport at Hailsham Community College, comments:

> 'Giving the pupils log books worked well. They had a clearer understanding of what was expected of them in each module of work and progressed more quickly. Setting personal targets allowed them to review their progress and consider their needs. Through the quality of the comments made in their log books, we knew that pupils were becoming more aware of their learning and their strengths and weaknesses.'

Pupils are kept in mixed-ability groups for the whole of Year 7 at Ninestiles School in Birmingham. Here, it is believed that accurate initial assessments over a diverse range of subjects are better accrued over a whole year before children are ability grouped at the start of Year 8.

During pupil/teacher interviews at the end of each module, children's competencies are recorded and their opinions as to the amount of progress they perceive themselves as having made, sought. At Ninestiles, assessment is a shared affair – with students involved at every stage. Goals and levels are clearly outlined on posters pinned up around the department. This signage is invaluable as not only does it help children see exactly where they are at, it is also a constant reminder of what they need to do to get to the next level, and how to go about doing it. At the time of writing the school is working on an ICT data board for PE. Here, both staff and pupils will be able to access visual evidence of exactly what is needed to reach a certain level. An online curriculum is also being planned, giving children and their parents the opportunity to access information relating to where they are at and where they are going.

Assessment for learning

Crichton Casbon, the Lead Consultant for PE with the QCA, has stated:

> 'The National Curriculum is more flexible than is often perceived. Often teachers look for instructions to inform their delivery, rather than focusing on what pupils have to achieve. It can be inclusive – it's just a question of interpretation.'

Assessment for learning is about working out what the needs of the group or the individual are and then deciding upon the best way for them to achieve their goal. It is less about records and more to do with reflecting on options, establishing priorities and raising student awareness of what progress actually is.

When high quality PE is taking place, throughout a lesson, questions related to learning are being asked by all involved. Teachers, other adults or leaders and, most crucially of all, pupils themselves will be involved in an ongoing process of observation and evaluation. What are we trying to achieve? How did we achieve it? What do we need to do to progress? Why did that go wrong? Is that task within my capabilities at the moment? Are there any alternative ways of doing it?

A hierarchy of questions is available and need to be targeted at the right people at the right time. As well as closed functional questions, alternatives require choices to be made. At other times, instances within an activity will need analysis or a whole set of outcomes need to be evaluated. The trick, however, is turning these questions into action – to give pupils the tools with which to unlock their own potential. In order to help them to get to the next level, some youngsters will need to understand or see for themselves what they need to do to progress. Others will be less independent and need prompting. Over time, however, operating in this fashion, with pupils expected to ask such things of their peers and themselves, levels of independence will rise and the speed of learning quicken.

Core tasks

To be inclusive, such an assessment process must be child centred – targeted around what an individual is able to do rather than at a set of pre-conceived, abstract outcomes. Core tasks for PE, provided by the QCA, can be adapted for use with children of all abilities.

Core tasks provide a sense of focus to both lessons and modules. Here, youngsters are piecing together their short-term learning, building towards something bigger. For children to access and engage any sport or physical activity, a diverse series of skills and tactics must be learnt. Often, however, individual concepts are learnt better in isolation – with youngsters able to focus on a specific set of requirements for a whole session. Organising modules around core tasks allows concepts to be learnt and extended individually, but also pieced together and related towards the overall goal.

Fielding drills can be boring. So, in one lesson, outlined below, in order to enthuse the group, they were given the option of extending their throwing, catching and intercepting skills by playing an adapted invasion game, in the midst of their striking and fielding module. However, the learning focus – clearly outlined at the start and reinforced throughout the session – was on the development of fielding skills not invasion principles. Questions like: 'How and when would you use these skills during a game of rounders?' or 'Next week we are going to play the core task again. How will what you have learnt today help you and your team do better?' were asked at various points throughout the lesson. Here, critical interventions can take the form of questions related to catching and throwing techniques and also how to stop a ball that is rolling along the ground.

A fielding lesson

Using a tennis ball, two teams of four scored points by hitting a target – a large cone – at the opposite end of a pitch which itself was divided into zones. No moving whilst in possession of the ball, no physical contact was allowed, and on a small pitch, underarm throwing below head height only! To prevent defenders from standing in front of the target and making it impossible to hit, one group came up with the idea of setting up a small 'no go' area around the target. Another decided that teams would be rewarded with a point for every five consecutive catches that they made. A third decided that every member of the group must touch the ball prior to a point being scored, while a few students, not particularly fond of learning through competition, preferred to practise their throwing and catching skills in the traditional way, designing for themselves a series of tests to encourage progress. This kind of approach encourages pupils to think creatively about how to develop skills and tactics independently.

While practising stopping a moving ball, one pupil in a wheelchair used a chute to roll the ball along the ground to a partner and then positioned

---

himself behind a long table, especially brought over from the school canteen, to receive the return. Obviously, he was unable to bend down and pick the ball up off the ground, but he could stop a moving ball – which was the focus of the lesson. His partner, an able-bodied child – didn't lose out because the focus of the session was not to do with rolling a ball along the ground. Although the disabled youngster, suffering from muscular dystrophy, lacked the strength to throw the ball in the air, re-arranging pairs into a group of three included him. While his partners threw the ball in the air to each other, they took it in turns to continue rolling it to him. The group did try positioning the chute on the edge of the table requiring a different sort of catching technique to be employed. One youngster in the school cricket team saw this going on and thought it would be an ideal way of practising slip catching.

Core tasks are adaptable and, if used with flexibility, facilitate creativity, innovation and personalised learning. But are they inclusive of the child with SEN, who may have difficulties remembering things learnt a week or two weeks ago? Videoing activity is of course one way of aiding memory. Similarly, before embarking on the current week's activity, one group could be asked to give a quick demonstration of what had been done the previous week, and could be asked, 'How can that be extended or applied to this week's activity?'

Similarly, one school used symbols to represent movements in a sequence, which were then laid out in front of the pupils to help them remember when to hop, jump, balance and roll. They were then asked, 'What will happen if you change the order of the symbols?'

Target setting

Working to core tasks enables both long and short-term targets to be set. To be inclusive, targets must be personalised and realistic – related to what the students themselves can do.

However, even at level 1, the National Curriculum talks of control and co-ordination. When compared to their able-bodied peers, some children, due to their physical disability or learning difficulty will never achieve this. Even some national champions in disability sport would be a level 1 or 2 if National Curriculum assessment levels were applied strictly.

Yet, if we take the earlier proviso that assessment should be about what a child can do, then it soon becomes apparent that some children with SEN can indeed reach exceptional levels of control and co-ordination. . . for them! An inclusive approach would assess an individual according to, and based on, an awareness of, *their* needs. The earlier example of the child in a wheelchair who can stop a moving ball easily is a case in point. Does it say anywhere in the National Curriculum that the ball has to be travelling along the ground? If the sport centric argument is used that in cricket, baseball and rounders the ball will travel along the floor, for severely disabled youngsters, their exit route may be into table cricket and so their PE experience is equally relevant! The CD-Rom accompanying this book gives details of table cricket, zone hockey and polybat.

Below, several ways of adapting disability sports to National Curriculum Programmes of Study, are given.

INCLUSION MODULES

	Programmes of study	Learning outcome
Acquiring and Developing	**KS3** • Refine and adapt existing skills • Develop them into specific techniques that suit different activities and perform these with consistent control	• Learn to use both types of ball in table cricket • Applying Boccia techniques to Throlf or bean bag games • Applying moving with a ball in zone hockey to floor lacrosse
	KS4 • Develop and apply advanced skills and techniques • Apply them in increasingly demanding situations	• Trying to hit harder targets in any of the games • Playing any of the games in either small-sided or competitive situations
Selecting and Applying	**KS3** • Use principles to plan and implement strategies in pair group and team activities • Modify and develop plans • Apply rules and conventions for different activities	• Try to outwit the opponent in Zone Hockey • Organise a small group as a team in Goalball • Use simple tactics in Boccia, or indeed any of the sports
	KS4 • Use advanced strategic concepts and principles • Apply these concepts in increasingly demanding situations • Apply rules and conventions for different activities	• Explain simple game plans for any of the games • Apply tactics learned in a game without help • Help to referee or score a game

	Programmes of study	Learning outcome
Evaluating/ Improving Knowledge/ Understanding of health and fitness	**KS3** • Be clear about what they want to achieve in their own work, and what they have actually achieved • Take the initiative to analyse their own and others' work using this information to improve its quality	• How to prepare for and recover from specific activities • How different types of activity affect specific aspects for their fitness • The benefits of regular exercise and good hygiene • How to go about getting involved in activities that are good for their personal and social health and well-being.
	KS4 • Make informed choices about what role they want to take in each activity • Judge how good a performance is and how to improve it • Prioritise and carry out these decisions to improve their own and others' performances • Develop leadership skills	• How preparation, training and fitness relate to and affect performance • How to design and carry out activity and training programmes that have specific purposes • The importance of exercise and activity to personal, social and mental health and wellbeing • How to monitor and develop their own training exercise and activity programmes in and out of school

Source: Primary and Secondary Inclusion modules

Adapted targets

A child-centred, generic approach to target setting facilitates inclusive teaching. Rather than thinking of the absolute mechanics related to the skill, thinking laterally about their application and how this relates to the pupil's movement capabilities enables appropriate targets, like the ones below, to be set (taken from Primary and Secondary Inclusion modules).

A pupil can run and jump by:

- walking/running – travel slowly/quickly by wheeling, shuffling, crawling or stepping

- hopping – moving part of the body, arm, leg from one side to the other, or hopping with both feet together

- wheelchair users can use arms to lift body into the air as an alternative to jumping

- moving body over low objects, mat or beam

- extending and contracting all or part of the body

- wheelchair users can also travel as far as possible with one push (long jump)

A pupil can travel with a ball by:

- holding the ball in their arms

- clutching the ball against their body

- balancing the ball on their lap/or other part of their body

- holding the ball in a receptacle

- pushing the ball along under control

- using equipment that is easier to hold (e.g. quoits, bean bags)

A pupil can, therefore, send the ball by:

- rolling or pushing it along the floor

- using a channel, tube, or gutter device

- rolling it at table-top level

- sending it using hands, feet, or any flat surface of the body (e.g. forearm)

- rolling it down the body from a seated position

- sending, using part of a wheelchair, sticks, crutches, rollator

- using a channel on the floor or table top

- releasing it in the most effective (rather than technical) arm position

A pupil can send and receive by:

- rolling the ball against a wall

- rolling it along a table top pushed against the wall, or lap tray with a 'rebounder'

- having it rolled rather than bounced
- having time to control the ball or not having to send the ball in one movement

A pupil can receive a ball by:

- stopping it with a part of the body, wheelchair, crutch, stick, rollator
- gathering the ball into the body using arms, legs or an implement
- gathering and controlling the ball using an enclosed space (e.g. corner)
- retrieving it using a string attached to the chair, wheelchair, racket
- having the ball replaced by a softer implement, e.g. a bean bag, koosh ball, partially deflated ball, no-bounce ball, spider ball

Pupils can kick a ball from a stationary position or while on the move, by:

- using a slower or faster moving ball
- kicking from a seated position
- using a crutch, stick or rollator to strike the ball
- using a partially deflated ball or bean bag for greater control

Pupils can strike a ball:

- with a bigger/smaller bat (larger or smaller striking area)
- by using a bigger/smaller ball (easier/harder to hit)
- from a stationary position on a T or cone
- using a rolled, bounced, delivery feed
- using a hand or forearm to strike
- using a bat glove or bat/racket attached to hand or arm

Case Study – Josh

Josh is a seventeen-year-old pupil with muscular dystrophy.

Because he has a degenerative complaint, Josh's capacity to progress in the conventional way is undermined. Put simply, the older he gets the weaker he is likely to become. Accessing activities becomes more difficult, making the idea of comparative assessment inappropriate. For a student like Josh, short-term personalised targets are essential.

Although Josh was a wheelchair-user, he had few problems engaging with the mainstream curriculum, lower down the school. All the usual adaptations – space, task, equipment and people – were used to assist him. As a keen sportsman, Josh also attended a club at the local special school where disability sports were played, and represented the club in inter-school competition.

As he got older and his complaint got hold of him, Josh indeed became weaker. Activities he previously enjoyed, he could no longer do. However, this did not mean that he could do nothing. Further adaptations were needed and in one such game – precision ramp ball – Josh won two gold medals at a national disability athletics competition. Precision ramp ball is an adaptation of the sort of target-throwing games seen in disability athletics settings. Designed especially for competitors with restricted upper body movement or very little strength, a ball is rolled down a ramp, scoring points depending on where it lands on the target.

At school, Josh's targets were based around regular re-appraisals of what he could do. His condition was deteriorating so rapidly that asking him to work towards something for the end of the year or even the end of the term was unrealistic. Monthly or even fortnightly skill development targets were set – as Josh was asked to vary ramp angles to achieve different distances, and utilise a variety of balls to contain greater control over his aiming. His knowledge of the rules of a game and its accompanying tactics was one area that was not diminishing and many of Josh's targets concerned how well he could pass information on to other pupils.

As a leader and a coach Josh continued to excel. At time of writing he is studying for A-levels at a nearby college of FE.

P scales

Adapted delivery and flexible interpretation should enable most children to access National Curriculum levels. However, in addition, QCA P scales are available for those youngsters working below this. P scales outline early learning and attainment prior to level 1 and can be used by teachers in the same way as the National Curriculum level descriptions to:

- decide which description best fits a pupil's performance over a period of time and in different contexts;

- develop or support more focused day-to-day approaches to ongoing teacher assessment by using the descriptions to refine and develop long, medium and short-term planning;

- track linear progress towards attainment at National Curriculum level 1;

- identify lateral progress by looking for related skills at similar levels across their subjects;

- record pupils' overall development and achievement, for example at the end of a year or a key stage.

Performance descriptions for P1 to P3 are common across all subjects, outlining the types and range of general performance that pupils with learning difficulties might characteristically demonstrate. From P 4 to P 8, levels are subject specific. (See CD for details.)

Photo: Simon Harris

What is progress?

Beyond simply improving performance, a whole host of other factors needs to be taken into account when measuring and assessing progress. Through involvement in PE and sport, a youngster can develop their social skills – increasing their ability to interact with their peers. Evidence also shows that success or enjoyment here could lead to the development of greater confidence and a more positive attitude to school life in general. Indicators of links between participation in physical activity and improvements in behaviour and academic standards have also been found. In many ways these 'life outcomes' are of far greater importance than whether a student can jump higher, run faster or hit a ball further than they could three weeks previously.

The PE and School Sport (PESS) website shows a variety of case studies demonstrating the wider impact of participation in physical activity. (see www.qca.org.uk/pess)

However, assessing the impact of physical activity on these life outcomes is more difficult and will always rely to some degree on subjective judgement – either the professional opinions of teachers and support staff, or the reliability of student comments. The example below illustrates this point well.

Example

Since Sarah started participating more regularly in over two hours of weekly physical activity, she seems happier and is contributing to class discussions to a greater extent across the curriculum and has made more friends.

But is it possible or indeed necessary to quantify an exact cause and effect relationship between the two? Will the youngster herself be aware of the exact reason for her developing confidence?

Yet those around her – her peers and her teachers will be able to spot the changes and, in this case, it is the outcome in terms of her quality of life, rather than the process which got her there, which is important.

For pure research reasons we could try taking away her weekly two-and-a-half hours to see if she regressed back into her old introverted self. Yet we are dealing with human beings here. So if the youngster is happier and more confident and an increased diet of physical activity may have contributed to this, do we need more than her word and, if that is unreliable or not forthcoming, the judgement of her teachers, to empirically prove it?

Case study – Rosie, a pupil with dyslexia and moderate learning difficulties

A Year 8 student, with dyslexia and moderate learning difficulties, Rosie had always struggled to access the academic curriculum. As she never caused much of a fuss, lack of SEN support at primary school meant that she was just left to soldier on, her language difficulties largely ignored. As she grew older and lagged further behind her peers, she lost interest in her schoolwork and began to show the first signs of disaffection from the whole educational process just after starting secondary school. 'What's the point?' she would tell herself. 'I can't do it. And people just think I'm thick.'

Yet Rosie had always been quite good at sport. She played cricket and football when nearby clubs delivered after-school sessions at her primary school. And at secondary school she started doing athletics and, when she played hockey in PE, was identified as having a great deal of potential and encouraged to go along to the local hockey club. Being very practical, Rosie liked sport. She was the sort of girl who would often cook dinner for her mum and sister at home, without burning the house down! The sort of girl who could shimmy up a tree without a second thought – while her friends looked on open-mouthed. Yet she hated school. She couldn't read and write properly. She had no future!

Even Rosie's favourite subject – PE – didn't offer her a way out academically. She might sail through the practical side of GCSE PE, especially if she could choose hockey and gymnastics as her focus activities, yet there was no way she would ever get through the written papers. The teachers knew this and told her mum that Rosie was 'unsuitable for GCSE PE'.

But what was the alternative? What provision would meet the needs of Rosie and others like her? At Rosie's school there was none. The new head teacher had a mission to lift the school out of special measures and could not see very far beyond league tables and Value Added scores. Institutional self-preservation meant that in his eyes, the needs of one 'little person' were insignificant compared to the bigger picture. School prestige was all that mattered. His own reputation was on the line!

Such a prevalent ethos meant that vocational or practical courses were viewed as poor relations to the GCSE, and all departments had been instructed not to waste time on them. Even though it was obvious that GCSE didn't suit all pupils, practical courses like the Certificate of Achievement in PE were dismissed, as they did not register as highly on the schools' performance data. But why is this? Are practical courses considered to be of less value? A vocational course, like the BTEC First in Sport, would have been perfect for Rosie. It is a mixture of practical, leadership opportunity and applied theory. Yet for her school, it would have meant staff training, departmental re-organisation and sparse resources pumped into what was after all considered by management to be a minor subject. Most importantly, it would have created a worrying precedent for a head teacher who didn't want to see his school flooded with 'unsuitable' vocational courses of this sort.

So Rosie continued to slip away from education and, in the end, stopped doing sport as well. Preferring to hang out on the street with mates, she became increasingly disaffected not just from school, but from home life. And all because her school could not offer her a pathway through which she could develop her particular abilities without having to rely on the academic competencies she didn't have.

While we remain obsessed with written tests, which by definition exclude many youngsters from achieving their potential in a subject like PE, simply because they struggle with literacy, youngsters like Rosie will continue not to fulfil their potential. Did Sir Alex Ferguson ask Wayne Rooney to sit a written exam before signing him for Manchester United? After crossing the finish line at the 2004 Olympics for the second time, did Kelly Holmes have to hand in a piece of coursework entitled 'Why I deserve to be a double Olympic champion' to the judges, before collecting her medal?

Yet if practical assessment using observation and subjective judgement is good enough for the highest profile sporting event in the world and a multi-million pound business like the Premiership, surely is it good enough for schools?

Listen to interviews conducted with some premiership footballers or, worse still, bump into them in a nightclub. You're not always dealing with rocket scientists here! Yet that does not diminish their understanding of the game they play, their ability to develop and apply skills, to evaluate their own performances and those of team-mates and opponents and to respond to them in training and, more importantly, during matches. As elite athletes, they will also have a highly developed sense of what to do to stay healthy and fit. But are you going to ask some of them to sit an Oxbridge entrance exam to prove it? Work in the last quarter century which has highlighted multiple intelligences, has established clear criteria for assessing physical intelligence. Why is our modern education system unable to take cognisance of this?

Of course, PE is more than just a practical subject. Thinking skills, decision-making processes and tactical awareness are all a major part of the subject. But as suggested earlier, for these to be made relevant – especially for children like Rosie – they need to be linked directly to practical aspects, not considered as abstract theories. So, rather than worrying about an anatomy course, Rosie should consider why a person with a particular physical make-up might be good at a certain sport. What sort of physical capacities would an oarsman, basketball player, or a fast bowler, need to develop, in order to excel? Rosie could do that. She could succeed, gain confidence, have a reason for being at school, for giving of her best, for working hard to secure a future for herself. Given these opportunities Rosie could be happier. Off the street. See a future for herself!

The best professional sportsmen and women are intelligent performers, working out what to do – in terms of technique, psychology, strategy and fitness – to enhance their performance and maximise their progress. Rosie could always explain what she was doing in PE and what she needed to do to progress to the next level. But ask her to write it down? Well, that was a different matter!

Public perception is always a barrier to the kind of innovation that would allow a wider range of 'level playing field' exam options. Fuelled by tabloid accusations, the indication is that the subjective judgements of teachers alone can't be relied upon to give an accurate indication of a pupil's performance. With management breathing down their neck, demanding higher standards, to give a pupil a low mark would be like turkeys voting for Christmas!

To help give the Rosies of this world an equal chance, what is needed is a way of increasing the validity of assessment procedures based around practical aspects and applied theory. Yes, they are accurate and inclusive. But how can we prove it?

Some schools have used video to provide evidence, and perhaps some sort of languages style 'oral' exam could be used to good effect. Ideally, however, these would be combined with and related to the practical elements of the exam, allowing students to make comments about, and demonstrate an understanding of, their performance and progress.

Lynne Spackman, a QCA consultant, states: 'The QCA are currently working with exam boards to support them in modernising their accreditation systems and bring them into line with twenty-first century PE and school sport.'

Maybe if the QCA were to flex their muscles with a bit more vigour and remind those on exam boards that tradition and the treasured ways of the past are not always the only way forward, then the life chances of students like Rosie could be increased considerably. This area is yet another example of how PE teachers concerned with inclusion must work for change if all pupils are to receive a fairer deal from schools.

CHAPTER 7

Managing Support

'We would like to be inclusive, but there are only three of us in the PE department so what can we do?'

'Creative group organisation and teaching methods? In theory, great! But we teach full timetables and have to manage groups of thirty on our own. All the TAs are working on the academic curriculum and the head teacher won't even consider re-arranging the timetable to allow us to work with smaller groups. After-school clubs? Yes we would like to offer a wider range and get more children involved, but we are under pressure to perform in the inter-schools competitions. If our football, netball, cross-country and athletics teams don't do well, it'll be our heads on the block!'

Traditionally, situations like this have led to pupils with special educational needs sitting on the sidelines, or worse still in the library, during PE lessons. These and many more children, unimpressed by traditional approaches and activities, have simply disengaged with physical activity as a result. However, departmental limitations need no longer constrain a school's ability to offer a positive experience in PE and sport for youngsters of all abilities. Today, an ethos of partnership, collaboration and co-operation means that the school gates need no longer mark the boundary of a pupil's educational world.

Starting from the proviso that a pupil's needs are the central determining factor of any plan, it then becomes a case of finding the most effective way of engaging that youngster and facilitating their progress and development. With so many agencies willing and able to give support to delivering both curricular and out of school hours learning for pupils with special educational needs, provision can now be area based, rather than school based. To manage this support, schools should ask themselves several questions:

- What is the best route for a young person to be guided along, so they can experience appropriate curricular and extra-curricular provision?

- In order to be more inclusive and engage pupils with SEN, what are we as school/PE staff deficient in, and how can we effectively access a range of partners and structures to help us overcome these problems?

- Who within the school will be responsible for co-ordinating support networks?

- How do we ensure that pupils with SEN pick up and use facilities which may involve travel beyond the local area?

After an evaluation such as this, the PE department might think rather differently about their capacity to manage and deliver a high quality, inclusive PE and sport experience for their children.

'Yes there are only three of us. But there's still a lot we can do. Adult-student ratio is our biggest barrier to inclusion. We need children to work on a wider range of activities and in smaller groups. Our School Sports Partnership is bidding for lottery funding to buy in external coaches, so once we start releasing our School Sport co-ordinator more regularly, we should be able to get in on that. A Junior Sports Leader's Award – great idea! Not only will that give us additional helpers for Key Stage 3 classes and clubs, but also it will give an alternative coaching and leadership route for older pupils, which should keep more of them interested for longer. At the Sports College down the road they are working with job seekers on something called the New Deal.[1] Not sure what it is – but it's worth finding out about. I think they've got one lad in charge of putting out all the equipment and using ICT to collate pupil attendance and assessment. That would save a lot of teaching time.'

'And what about the local sports clubs – I read the other day that national governing bodies are giving them assistance and in some cases funding, to go out into the community and establish links with schools. But there are so many, which ones shall we contact? Perhaps the local council's sports development team will know the good ones who are able to provide quality coaches to work at school. The council also know about local volunteer groups – maybe these groups might be able to find some people who want to get involved after school. There's a disability sport officer based at the council too. Perhaps she might be able to give us some ideas of how to get more of our disabled pupils involved, like they do at the special school down the road. The special school! Of course! They'll have some fantastic ideas on how we can involve our SEN pupils in PE lessons and out-of-school-hours clubs. Didn't I hear that the LEA had just given them some funding to provide an outreach service?'

These are just a few examples of how thinking beyond the confines of the school and what the personnel of the PE department have the time for, can increase a school's capacity to deliver high quality, inclusive PE. With some, or all, of these individuals and organisations on board – a wider range of activities can be delivered, and staff directed to work with smaller groups.

Funding

Often, budgetary constraints will not permit the employment of extra staff or the wholesale transport of pupils to and from off-site activity. However, other funding streams can be dipped into.

Awards for All

Although schools may still apply for grants of up to £10,000 through Awards for All to organise and extend extra-curricular provision, Awards for All is no longer the open treasure chest it once was. Criteria for application is how much more rigid and, since changes introduced during 2004, schools are no longer a priority organisation for funding. On top of this, the amount released by Sport England for sports-based projects has been slashed considerably.

Set up in 1998 to allow non-profit making organisations to apply for lottery funding for specific projects, Awards for All aims to support community activity, through its grants which will:

- extend access and participation by encouraging more people to become actively involved in projects and activities;

- increase skill and creativity by supporting activities that help develop people and organisations, encourage talent and raise standards;

- improve the quality of life by supporting local projects that improve people's opportunities, welfare, environment or facilities.

To apply, a school must first design a project with a community focus that corresponds to Awards for All's national and regional priorities.

These priorities can be ascertained by accessing Awards for All's website on www.awardsforall.org.uk. and on the map click on the country of choice, followed by the region of your choice. Click on regional focus to see what the area's priorities are. Assessors will look for evidence of real Partnerships with outside organisations such as sports clubs, while wanting reassurance of the involvement of senior management in the application process, to ensure the school takes ownership of its project. In the past, some schools have merely been the passive recipients of services, paid for by grants, but without making the activity part of school life.

It is important to remember that *Awards for All will not fund curriculum activity*, as lottery money cannot be used for activities that are part of statutory obligations. Although it would be unrealistic to expect that equipment bought for the purposes of setting up a basketball club would not be used during PE lessons, an application designed to restock the school's PE cupboard, will be rejected.

What Awards for All will fund, however, is transport to and from sporting and other activities. A major issue for many children with special educational needs (particularly those in special schools) accessing after-school clubs is their reliance on school transport to get them home. However, even though an Awards for All grant will help overcome this problem initially, innovative thinking is needed to sustain such a project, long term.

Sports wheelchairs are lighter, quicker and more manoeuvrable than other wheelchairs

Case study – Sam, a pupil with spina bifida and hydrocephalus

Sam, an eleven-year-old girl from Tamworth, has spina bifida and hydrocephalus. As she is a keen and budding athlete, Sam was provided with a sports wheelchair by Whizz-Kidz. One of a number of charities set up to assist children with physical disabilities and other special educational needs, Whizz-Kidz target their support at youngsters under the age of eighteen, for whom the NHS is unable to provide much needed mobility equipment, training and advice. (See the Whizz-Kidz website: www.whizz-kidz.org.uk)

Sam loved her wheelchair so much that when she recently grew out of it, she applied for a new one so she could carry on enjoying sport with her friends. Her new wheelchair is light and manageable, was built specifically for her and is great for indoor and outdoor sports. She also uses it as her 'everyday' wheelchair so it meets all her needs – which is a good thing, as taking two wheelchairs in the car was a bit tricky for Mum, with four kids!

Over the last five years, Sam has gained in confidence dramatically. She has used her sports wheelchair on her school sports day, and in wheelchair basketball games and weekly athletic sessions. Her latest hobby is non-contact boxing, which is good not only for her fitness and co-ordination but also a great way for her to make friends. Sam's sports wheelchair has given her a positive attitude towards her disability and having to use a wheelchair, and has also allowed her to enjoy many new hobbies.

Sam's mother says:

> The wheelchair has given Sam independence and a brighter outlook for the future. Without it she would have probably have had to be pushed around in her wheelchairs for the rest of her life, never experiencing the freedom and independence that most of us take for granted.

Parents or carers of disabled children can contact the charity, which will then send out a trained therapist to assess the child's needs and lifestyle before considering the type of equipment best suited to them. Equipment is free (although those who can afford it may be asked to make a contribution towards costs) and can be designed to meet the specific needs of the young person.

Sports development support

Sports development officers, employed by both local authorities and national governing bodies of sport, can provide a great deal of support for schools. As well as providing access to good quality clubs and coaches, with whom schools can forge partnerships, sports development professionals can also help PE departments engage youngsters with special educational needs.

Today's sports development personnel – urged on by their political and organisational masters – are beginning to use initiatives and strategies more innovatively in order to meet local needs. Not always, but often, due to differences of organisational practice and ethos, sports development professionals have found it difficult to work with schools in any sort of meaningful and efficient way. Yet they are required to do so and are usually very welcoming to any teacher or school who shows a desire to get involved with them. Watch out for many meetings and endless forms to fill in as the 'paperwork' culture still exists to a certain extent, but there are now many more people in sports development with the wherewithal to 'do' as well as plan. They can be of valuable assistance in many ways.

In South Gloucestershire, a collaborative approach to the organisation and delivery of school sport has reaped dividends. Based in one central office, the sports development team, the LEA PE adviser and one of the Partnership Development Managers from the School Sports Partnership, co-ordinate matters centrally, under the banner of 'South Gloucestershire Sports Team'. Not only does this provide a single point of access for teachers, parents and children, but access to schools for outside organisations – such as national governing bodies, sports clubs, the Active Sports Team (who occupy the other side of the office) and specialist support services for children with special educational needs – is made easier.

A Gloucestershire charity supporting physically disabled adults, Paul's Place, was given funding by Awards for All to extend their sports provision to youngsters aged 11 to 18. (Go to www.paulsplace.org.uk for details of the charity.) An initial letter drop around local schools offering in-school taster sessions and invitations to subsequent community activity for children failed to produce any interest. Inundated with other correspondence, teachers simply didn't prioritise or even acknowledge, what was to them a new and unfamiliar group. Soon afterwards the charity contacted the South Gloucestershire Sports Team who advised them to change track. In setting up several community days, the team's physical activity consultant, Andy Holt, had been charged with visiting schools to drum up interest. Andy, a former local teacher and school sport co-ordinator, had a network of personal contacts with key individuals in schools which he utilised to encourage more to take notice and more children to take part. In order to extend provision and engage more children, the Sports Team also organised activities for children with learning disabilities to run at the same time and place as those targeting physically disabled youngsters. Clearly, personal contact, especially when that person is a subject specialist, pays richer dividends than mailshots, which are in danger of been consigned to the bin under the tag 'junk mail'.

All national governing bodies of sport have equity targets, set for them by government, through Sport England. This means that they need to secure and sustain the involvement of more girls, youngsters from ethnic minority and disadvantaged backgrounds, and children with physical and learning disabilities, in their chosen sport. To keep the money coming from central government, they are also required to work with schools. Sports-specific programmes of activities, equipment and specially trained coaches are available for schools. It's just a case of making contact and finding them.

Launched at Highbury Stadium early in 2004, the FA's three-year £90,000 Soccability Scheme aims to provide people of any age or ability, a pathway into the sport. (For details of the scheme, see www.thefa.com/TheFA/ EthicsAndSportsEquity/) Over 400 schools can expect free equipment and coaching packs to assist the delivery of the game to disabled children. These ideas, based around the inclusion spectrum, are also ideal when designing activities for children with learning disabilities or other special educational needs. In order to establish routes into community football, county development officers will then work with clubs who, to retain Charter Standard status, will need to provide a workable plan for including disabled players, coaches, referees and administrators within their set-ups. The establishment of 50 'Ability Counts' clubs to compete regularly all around the country, is also part of this plan.

Jeff Davis of the FA Disability Working Group states:

> England now have six different disability teams – blind, partially sighted, cerebral palsy, amputees, learning disabilities and deaf. But a thriving top end needs strong grass roots. A fourteen-year-old youngster with cerebral palsy, living on the Isle of Wight, has to have a clear pathway to access coaching and the chance to compete at a level suitable to his ability.

The England and Wales Cricket Board (ECB) is also working to break down barriers to the inclusion of children with special educational needs into our national summer game. In 2001 it launched its National Strategy for Disabled Cricket as an integral part of its overall plan to make England the top cricketing nation by 2007. (Copies are available to download from http://www.ecb.co.uk/ ecb/development/development-disabilities) Following the same structure, it outlines seven steps from school playground to test arena and pledges to provide pathways along which young disabled cricketers can progress. In its quest, the ECB is supported by a large number of organisations that provide cricket for people with specific physical impairments and learning disabilities. Extensive coverage of cricket for disabled people can be found at www.cricketworld.com the online version of *Cricket World* magazine. Contact 01476 561944 for details. Not least of these organisations are the Lords Taverners, a charity to whom applications for equipment and, in some cases, financial assistance can be made by schools wishing to develop opportunities for children – particularly those with special educational needs – to play cricket. (Details at www.lordstaverners.org or on 020 7821 2828/9.)

In 2001 the *ECB National Strategy for Disabled Cricket* stated:

> We aim to ensure every disabled student of secondary school age has the opportunity to develop their respective range of skills, understanding, enjoyment and appreciation of the game.

Sixth Annual Lord's Taverners National Table Cricket Final – Tuesday 13th July 2004.

In a tense final at Lord's, Victoria School in Poole successfully defended their title against Wilson Stuart from Birmingham.

'Table cricket is great fun and we practise all year round. It feels incredible to win again – here's to a third year!' Victoria school captain, Garry Hobbs, after receiving the trophy from Lord's Taverners Table Cricket Ambassador, actor Ricky Groves – East Enders' Garry Hobbs.

Forty-four schools competed in regional heats, held at county cricket grounds and other venues all over the country during the summer term. The winners got the opportunity to play an innovative, competitive team game designed especially for youngsters with physical impairments or co-ordination difficulties, at the spiritual home of world cricket.

'This is the second year running I have been to the competition. It is a great way to make new friends. I also play boccia, which is played at the Paralympics and take part in athletics, so you do get to see other players outside of table cricket. However I really like table cricket because you can control the batting and the bowling. When you're up in front of your team you feel really nervous but it's worth it for the excitement of being in a competition like this. The best things about it are meeting new people – and of course, winning!' (Stacey Gallagher – Year 8 student from Bruntcliffe School, Leeds)

Source: *Cricket World*

Inclusion is high on the agenda of 'the powers that be' in Nottinghamshire, and has led to an amalgamation of support services for SEN children. An inclusive PE and sport group – including representatives from education, access, physiotherapy, a special school head teacher, the LEA PE adviser, two parent governors of children with SEN and the principal officer from the Sports Disability Unit – now co-ordinates matters relating to provision and inclusion throughout the county. Yet LEA policy means that it has its work cut out!

An LEA insisting that schools meet the needs of as wide a range of abilities as possible made it extremely difficult for a child to get the statement they needed for a place at a special school. As a result, a large number of pupils with special educational needs within Nottinghamshire schools were getting a raw deal when it came to PE and sport. Consultation in local schools raised awareness of various issues and barriers to the participation of youngsters in mainstream PE and sport. While negative experiences were causing a high drop-out rate in school, there were negligible community sports opportunities for disabled people, few people trained to include disabled youngsters in PE and sport, and a lack of accessible transport.

Realising that there was a gap in provision, a new project – 'Inside Out' – was formulated. In April 2003, a project officer, Carol Halpin, was assigned to support and establish strategies to improve inclusion for disabled pupils and pupils on the SEN registers of mainstream schools, in PE and sport. Her role has been to:

- deal with schools' enquiries on issues relating to PE and sport and co-ordinate appropriate support from outside agencies;

- provide an adapted PE and sport curriculum, accessible to all pupils;

- assess individual needs;

- provide information and links to other support networks;

- provide Ambassadors of Disability Sport[2];

- provide accessible and inclusive sport equipment.

Although spending much of her time in schools, Carol Halpin is based in the County Council's Sports Disability Unit – a stone's throw from both the City Ground and Trent Bridge. She is also part of an inclusive PE and sport group who manage the Inside Out project. Regular contact with a wide variety of agencies and individuals not only helps the liaison process, but also makes it easier for Carol to take a more holistic view of any situation she encounters. Being physically detached enables a person with a broad remit to take a child-centred perspective and not to get bogged down by the day-to-day realities of a particular school.

Sadly, inclusion is not valued as highly everywhere, as it is in Nottinghamshire. But even in a place where tradition rules and the attitude has been to ignore the implications of inclusion – things can change.

In special schools, there are experienced professionals with many years' experience of adapting both curriculum content and delivery to meet a wide range of needs. They are simply too good a 'resource' to ignore.

Alongside his role as Head of PE at Wilson Stuart Special School in Birmingham, Simon Harris is also employed by his LEA as a consultant. The

Photo: Simon Harris

focus of his outreach work with local schools (and further afield for those who can afford to buy in his time) is how to help schools improve their capacity to deliver PE and sport in a more inclusive manner. As well as trying to increase awareness of a wider range of specific needs and expand schools' knowledge of the issues affecting children with SEN and their ability to access PE, he also suggests practical solutions and offers advice on how to utilise and adapt a variety of strategies. At a breakfast club run at a nearby secondary school, one pupil with cerebral palsy would sit and watch while the others played table tennis. On discovering that the sport was an area of focus for the school, Simon Harris introduced the breakfast club organiser to the game 'polybat'. With similar rules, the youngster was then able to join in and enjoy playing alongside his peers. Another PE department was panicking at the prospect of four children with physical disabilities joining their Year 7. Showing them basic adaptions to mainstream activities – for instance how plastic chutes could be used to send and receive, and how for a child with brittle bones, invasion games could be modified to prohibit marking within three feet of an opponent – took the pressure off and gave teachers confidence to engage these pupils.

Simon Harris explains:

'Initially I meet with the pupil, assess their needs and attitude towards PE. From here, in discussion with the relevant teacher or perhaps the Head of Department, schemes of work are appraised and if necessary adapted. It's all about getting people to focus on what children can do, not what they can't do. From this it is possible to plan a block of work which can facilitate inclusive teaching.'

Simon's role as an LEA consultant provides a model which could be copied almost anywhere in the UK, providing the will exists.

A diverse network of supporting organisations and individuals is out there for schools to tap into – but big questions remain unanswered. Who will organise it within a school? Who will make sure relevant information reaches PE teachers? Who will make sure that the school is aware of the potential avenues of funding and support and, more importantly, how to access them successfully?

At Dayncourt School in Nottinghamshire, a Teaching Assistant has taken on this role. As well as offering practical support in PE lessons, Richard Whitehead, himself an international standard disabled athlete, works within the community as a sports development officer. Whereas a SENCO or a Head of PE may not have the time to commit to what would be only one of many areas of responsibility, for Richard it is his main priority. He has designated time within which he can accrue relevant knowledge, pursue potential partners and arrange suitable training. In regular meetings with both PE and SEN departments he can facilitate the sort of two-way dialogue that is essential if the needs of youngsters are to be understood and then acted upon.

Case study – Alex, a pupil with cerebral palsy

Alex, a Year 7 child with cerebral palsy was not accessing PE at his primary school. Walking with sticks, he couldn't do anything involving ball handling and often found himself on the sidelines during lessons. To him, PE was simply something other people did!

On arriving at Dayncourt, Alex once again found it difficult. He had extremely low confidence as regards his own capacity to take part and, initially, even staff at the sports college found it difficult to adapt their activities so he could join in.

The turning point came when Richard Whitehead used his contacts with the County Council Sports Disability Unit to get hold of a sports wheelchair for Alex. At once, a youngster who had struggled to move around during lessons was not only mobile, but could use his hands. Suddenly, a whole host of hitherto impossible possibilities were open to him. PE staff were now more confident in adapting activities. Playing basketball for the first time, a rule was introduced whereby every member of the team had to touch the ball prior to their team scoring a point. Focusing on 'man-to-man' marking in another lesson saw the smallest members of the class appointed to oppose Alex. Introducing these modifications from the start, rather than halfway through a lesson when it was realised that 'the kid in the wheelchair can't do it', prevented Alex from feeling he was being singled out. Similarly, others didn't think that their game was 'being mucked around with just cos Alex couldn't do it'.

For Alex the presence within the school of a person able to empathise with the issues and problems he was facing in attempting to access PE and sport, helped him enormously. At last, someone who actually understood, was telling Alex, a child with little use of his legs, that Alex could do it. A guy with even less use of his own legs was the living proof that it was possible for Alex and others with similar difficulties, to succeed. Even greater is that effect when the adult doing the persuading happens to have played sledge hockey for Great Britain, cricket for England, swum in two world youth games and run the 2004 New York Marathon!

Teaching assistants

The potential for the involvement of a host of outside agencies and individuals in a subject like PE and sport, not to mention the possibility of Junior Sports Leaders assisting with lessons lower down the school, makes the role of TAs somewhat less crucial than in subjects where such assistance is not available. Nevertheless, a Teaching Assistant with the right sort of knowledge, experience and attitude, can play a major role.

TAs employed to support individual pupils (usually those who have a statement of special educational needs) will know the child very well, and will be a useful source of information about exactly what the pupil can and cannot do and, hopefully, an ally if persuasion has to be used to get the child to 'have a go' at new activities. Independence is an increasingly recognised issue for pupils with SEN who have a TA 'attached' to them – there can be a powerful mothering instinct at work to 'protect' the child; fortunately, this is now being addressed by good training. (Disabled athletes travel all over the world to play sport. They don't need pity and sympathy – they need understanding and opportunity.)

It may be appropriate however, for the PE staff to offer some specific INSET for any TAs they are lucky enough to meet in the course of their lessons. It will certainly be valuable to discuss with them what their particular contribution might be.

The aim of TA support should be to use a range of strategies before, during and/or after each lesson to:

- facilitate maximum participation in and access to PE and sport for pupils with SEN

- encourage pupils to remain focused and on task

- reduce the incidence of disruptive behaviour

- foster greater pupil independence

- increase pupils' confidence and self-esteem

- raise attainment

Staff in the PE department may negotiate with TAs to clarify more specific roles. These may include:

- clarifying and explaining instructions, questions, tasks

- keeping pupils on task

- overseeing the setting up and care of equipment

- reading or helping pupils to read written material

- assisting pupils in practice

- monitoring pupil behaviour

- differentiating tasks and materials

- encouraging and praising pupils

- helping pupils to work towards their IEP targets

- keeping teachers informed of difficulties encountered by pupils

Case study – Kerri, a girl with moderate learning difficulties

Kerri, a girl with moderate learning difficulties, was in tears after her first PE lesson at secondary school. Her class had been given a striking and fielding task to do, which was used as a formative assessment of initial capabilities in that subject area. But Kerri had hated every second of it. She was adamant that she was never doing PE again. In fact it took several hours of persuading from her parents that evening before she was even prepared to come to school the next day.

It transpired that, at her primary school, Kerri had been allowed to opt out of PE whenever she felt like it. So, when during the aforementioned lesson she had been asked to take part in a small-sided game, independently – she simply couldn't cope. At primary school she only had to look sad or 'turn on the waterworks' and a sympathetic adult would take her to one side to find out what was the matter. She 'had it off to a tee'. Quite a cunning avoidance strategy really! Listening to and then following instructions – What was the point when you only had to pull a face and someone would come and tell you what to do again?

When her new PE teacher spoke to her before her next PE lesson she discovered that the last time Kerri had played a similar striking game was at primary school. When it was her turn to bat, the class TA had stood alongside her, helping her hold the bat. As the ball came down they swung the bat together and 'There you go! Well done, Kerri' And this was an able-bodied child with moderate learning difficulties!

Kerri had simply been a bit worried that she might not be able to hit the ball and knew if she played the sympathy card then she would either get out of having her go or would have someone do it for her. Although she might have been relieved initially, it was soon discovered that Kerri would have been quite capable of hitting the ball on her own.

As the module progressed, strategies to increase the student's independence were introduced. As her levels of self-confidence regarding her own capacity to achieve anything independently were so low, this had to be done gradually. Kerri was part of a group who initially struck the ball from a T, rather than having it fed to them by a teammate or in the case of the more able group, an opponent. She liked the fact that she was not the only one to be hitting the ball in this way and that the targets set for each group weren't shared with the other group. She didn't like to stand out or let others realise she wasn't as good as them. She also enjoyed the activity cards her group was given, which had diagrams to remind her what she had to do. Slowly Kerri began to improve her skills. She found that asking her team mates to roll, rather than throw the ball to her, made it easier for her to stop, when fielding and by the end of the module she was able to strike a moving ball with some consistency.

Now in year eight, Kerri still wouldn't class PE as her favourite subject and she still doesn't attend any after school or lunchtime clubs. However, she doesn't try and get out of doing it anymore, there are no tears and now that she has realised that she can do things for herself, she can be quite spiky towards the unsuspecting teacher or TA who offers her advice, when she appears to be struggling.

'I can do it you know!'

- suggesting to the teacher ways in which pupils could access the PE curriculum more easily

- developing positive relationships with pupils

- contributing information about pupils' progress

Specialist PE Teaching Assistants could be a great asset. If sufficient funding becomes available, the workload agreement to remodel the school workforce could provide exactly the sort of scope for innovation that PE departments need to be more inclusive in their delivery. Alongside the Richard Whitehead's of this world – specialists with the knowledge of PE and understanding of SEN issues – sports coaches, or even other adults with an interest in sport or simply a playing background, could be trained as PE-specific TAs.

As well as supporting individual children within lessons and liaising with the SEN department, such individuals, especially if they were to be allowed flexible working hours, could be involved in:

- Leadership, coaching and officiating in after-school clubs and matches

- Collating information about pupil participation and progress. This could involve responsibility for producing interactive displays to assist and inform learning

- Administration of bookings, courses, fixtures and travel

Notes

1 New Deal Sport in Schools is being organised jointly by the Government through Jobcentre plus as part of their wider New Deal programme and the Youth Sport Trust as an extension of their Specialist Sports College and School Sport Co-ordinator programme. The aim is to give unemployed people

the chance to work as Sports Technicians developing transferable skills, while at the same time enhancing the quality of PE and sport within a school. Contact the local job-centre for details of how to get involved.

2 Ambassadors of Disability Sport are athletes that have achieved at world class competition in disability sport who are qualified coaches. Funded by the Children's Fund, they can be used at presentations to raise disability awareness, to assist in PE lessons and talk to pupils about their achievements.

Useful Contacts

National governing bodies of sport

All England Netball Association – 01462 442344/www.england-netball.co.uk
Amateur Rowing Association (ARA) – 020 8237 6700/www.ara-rowing.org
Amateur Swimming Association – 01509 618 700/www.britishswimming.org
Badminton Association of England – 01908 268400/www.baofe.co.uk
Baseball Softball UK and major League Baseball – 0207453 7055/www. BaseballSoftballUK.com
British Cycling Federation – 0870 871 2000/www.bcf.uk.com
British Gymnastics – 0845 1297129/www.british-gymnastics.org
British Triathlon Association – 01509 226161/www.britishtriathlon.org
England and Wales Cricket Board (ECB) – 0207432 1200/www.ecb.co.uk
England Squash – 0161 231 4499/www.squash.co.uk
English Basketball Association – 0113 236 1166/www.basketballengland.org.uk
English Lacrosse Association – 0161 834 4582/www.englishlacrosse.co.uk
English Table Tennis Association – 01424 722525/www.etta.co.uk
English Volleyball Association – 0115 981 6324/www.volleyballengland.org
Football Association – 0207745 4601/www.the-fa.org
Hockey England – 01908 544644/www.hockeyonline.co.uk
Lawn Tennis Association – 0207831 7000/www.lta.org.uk
National Rounders Association – 0114 2480357/www.NRA-rounders.co.uk
Rugby Football League – 0113 2329111/www.sporting-life.com/rugbyleague
Rugby Football Union – 0208892 2000/www.rfu.com
The Golf Foundation – 01920 876200/www.golf-foundation.org
UK Athletics – 0870 998 6800/www.ukathletics.net

English Federation of Disability Sport www.efds.co.uk – this website contains numerous links to a host of organisations involved in the promotion of sporting and other opportunities for young people with disabilities.

Sports councils within the UK

Sports Council for Northern Ireland – www.sportni.org
Sports Council for Wales – www.sports-council-wales.co.uk
Sport England – www.sportengland.org
sportscotland – www.sportscotland.org.uk
UK Sport – www.uksport.gov.uk

Professional subject organisations

British Association of Advisers and Lecturers in Physical Education (BAALPE)
www.baalpe.org
Physical Education Association of the United Kingdom (PEAUK)
www.pea.uk.com

National sports organisations

British Olympic Association (BOA) – www.olympics.org.uk
British Paralympic Association (BPA) – www.paralympics.org.uk
British Sports Trust (BST) – www.bst.org.uk
Central Council of Physical Recreation – (CCPR) www.ccpr.org.uk
National Council for School Sport – www.schoolsport.freeserve.co.uk
sports coach UK – www.sportscoachuk.org S
Sportsmatch – www.sportsmatch.co.uk
Women's Sports Foundation – www.wsf.org.uk

Other useful links

Child Protection in Sport Unit (CPSU) – www.sportprotects.org.uk
4Children – www.4children.org.uk
DfES publications – 0845 602 2260 – dfes@prolog.uk.com
Education Extra – www.educationextra.org.uk
General Teaching Council (GTC) – www.gtce.org.uk
Qualifications and Curriculum Authority (QCA) – www.qca.org.uk
Specialist Schools Trust (SST) – www.specialistschoolstrust.org.uk
Sporting Equals – www.cre.gov.uk/speqs/
Teacher Training Agency (TTA) – www.useyourheadteach.gov.uk
Youth Sport Trust – www.youthsporttrust.org

References

DfES (2002) *Success for All: Reforming Further Education and Training.* London: DfES.

DfES (2004) *High Quality PE & Sport for Young People.* London: DfES.

DfES (2004) *Removing Barriers to Achievement: The Government's Strategy for SEN.* London: DfES.

First Steps (2004) Youth Sport Trust in conjunction with Contin You, the Peter Harrison Foundation and the English Federation of Disability Sport.

Stakes, R. and Hornby, G. (2000) *Meeting Special Needs in Mainstream Schools: A Practical Guide for Teachers.* London: David Fulton.

Vaughan, M. (2000) *The Index for Inclusion: Developing Learning and Participation in Schools.* CSIE.

Winnick, J. (1982) *Adapted PE & Sport.* Adapted for the UK in 1997 by collaboration between the Youth Sport Trust, Liverpool Community College and the British Paralympic Association.

Appendices

Evaluating Quality Provision – Indicators of High Quality PE/sport

Year group	
Period of focus	
Lead member of staff	
General impression as to overall focus of group related to indicators	
Specific areas of strength	
Specific areas of weakness	
Names of children exceeding expectations	
Names of children not meeting expectations	
Names of children making exceptional progress	
Names of children making little or no progress	
Ideas for improving/sustaining progress	

High Quality PE and Sport: Individual Checklist (SEN)

NAME: YEAR GROUP:

NATURE OF SEN/PROBLEMS OF ACCESS TO PHYSICAL ACTIVITY:

EXISTING INTERESTS:

On a sliding scale of 1–10 (1 being poor, through below satisfactory, satisfactory – good – right through to 10 as excellent), how does the student rate for each of these indicators?

INDICATOR OF HIGH QUALITY PE AND SPORT	RATING
● Committed, making PE and sport a central part of life in and out of school	
● Know and understand what they are trying to achieve and how to go about doing it	
● Understand that PE and sport are an important part of an active, healthy lifestyle	
● Has the confidence to get involved	
● Has the skills and control to take part	
● Willingly takes part in a range of group and individual activities	
● Can think about what they are doing and make appropriate decisions for themselves	
● Wants to improve and achieve in relation to own abilities	
● Has the stamina, suppleness and strength to keep going	
● Enjoys PE, school and community sport	

Strategic Planner

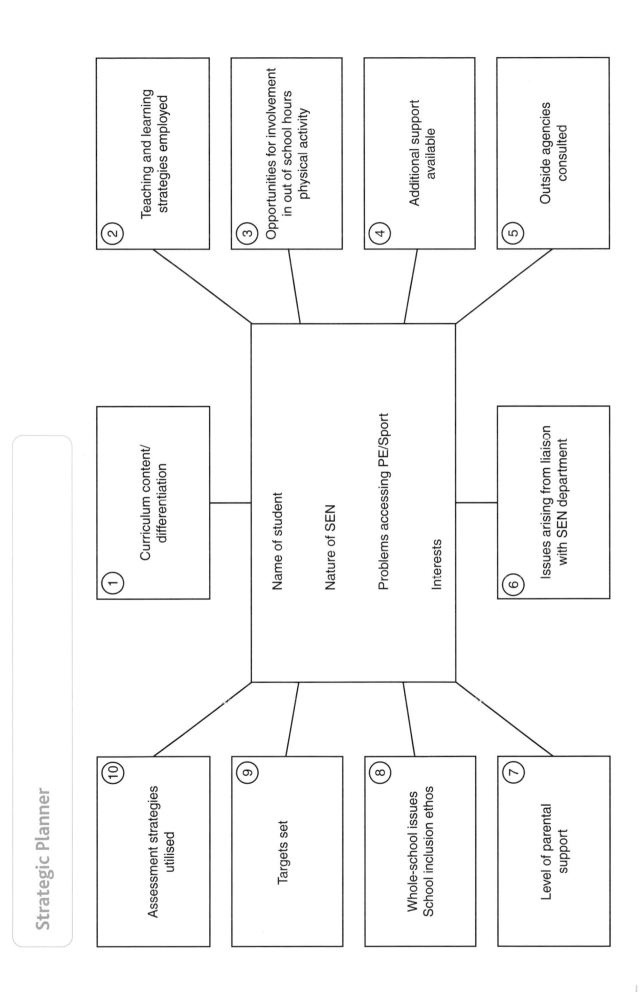

Name of student

Nature of SEN

Problems accessing PE/Sport

Interests

1. Curriculum content/differentiation
2. Teaching and learning strategies employed
3. Opportunities for involvement in out of school hours physical activity
4. Additional support available
5. Outside agencies consulted
6. Issues arising from liaison with SEN department
7. Level of parental support
8. Whole-school issues School inclusion ethos
9. Targets set
10. Assessment strategies utilised

P Scales

QCA P scales are available for those youngsters working below National Curriculum level 1. P scales outline early learning and attainment prior to level 1 and can be used by teachers in the same way as the National Curriculum level descriptions to generate targets and focus assessment opportunities.

P1 (i) Pupils encounter activities and experiences. They may be passive or resistant. They may show simple reflex responses, *for example startling at sudden noises or movements.* Any participation is fully prompted.

P1 (ii) Pupils show emerging awareness of activities and experiences. They may have periods when they appear alert and ready to focus their attention on certain people, events, objects or parts of objects, *for example turning briefly towards fast-moving group activity.* They may give intermittent reactions, *for example sometimes turning away from people or objects moving close to them.*

P2 (i) Pupils begin to respond consistently to familiar people, events and objects. They react to new activities and experiences, *for example showing surprise when moving into an outdoor environment.* They begin to show interest in people, events and objects, *for example patting at footballs brought towards them.* They accept and engage in coactive exploration, *for example moving about in the swimming pool with the support of a member of staff.*

P2 (ii) Pupils begin to be proactive in their interactions. They communicate consistent preferences and affective responses, *for example smiling in dance or movement activities.* They recognise familiar people, events and objects, *for example gesturing or vocalising in a particular way on arrival at the poolside.* They perform actions, often by trial and improvement, and they remember learned responses over short periods of time, *for example pushing away a ball when it is repeatedly rolled towards them.* They co-operate with shared exploration and supported participation, *for example being guided in creating patterns of movement.*

P3 (i) Pupils begin to communicate intentionally. They seek attention through eye contact, gesture or action. They request events or activities, *for example pointing to a particular piece of PE equipment.* They participate in shared activities with less support. They sustain concentration for short periods. They explore materials in increasingly complex ways, *for example tapping one item of equipment with another.* They observe the results of their own actions with interest, *for example dabbling their hands in the swimming pool and attending to the effects.* They remember learned responses over more extended periods, *for example bouncing up and down on a trampette.*

P3 (ii) Pupils use emerging conventional communication. They greet known people and may initiate interactions and activities, *for example pushing a ball towards a peer or adult.* They can remember learned responses over increasing periods of time and may anticipate known events, *for example beginning to move* *when the music starts.* They may respond to options or choices with actions or gestures, *for example moving towards one outdoor activity rather than another.* They actively explore objects and events for more extended periods, *for example moving around a space and encountering a range of objects or obstacles.* They apply potential solutions systematically to problems, *for example reaching out a foot or a hand to intercept a moving ball.*

Performance descriptions in physical education

From level P4 to P8, many believe it is possible to describe pupils' performance in a way that indicates the emergence of skills, knowledge and understanding in PE. The descriptions provide an example of how this can be done.

P4 Pupils' movement patterns are established and they perform single actions, *for example rolling, running, jumping or splashing.* They respond to simple commands, *for example 'stop'.* They recognise familiar pieces of equipment, *for example a ball or hoop.* They show awareness of cause and effect, *for example knocking down skittles.*

P5 Pupils link two actions in a sequence, *for example crawling and walking, or climbing and jumping.* They follow simple instructions although they may need the support of symbols or other prompts. They explore a variety of movements and show some awareness of space. They understand some basic concepts, *for example taking big and little steps in movement activities or placing big and small balls in different baskets.* They take turns with a partner or in a small group. They recognise and collect, on request, familiar pieces of equipment, *for example a mat to lie on or a hoop to jump into.*

P6 Pupils work in pairs and in small groups co-operatively, although they may need support to follow instructions and keep on task. They move in a variety of ways, *for example slowly and quickly.* They link movements in a simple sequence, although they may require support to do this. They recognise small and large apparatus and use it with some basic control. They throw and kick a ball, but lack direction.

P7 Pupils express themselves through repetitive and simple sequences and movement patterns. Their control and co-ordination skills are developing, *for example they kick a ball towards a target or throw a ball to a partner.* They listen to instructions and stop and start with some accuracy. They work closely in pairs, trios or small groups. They share and wait their turn. They are aware of the changes that happen to their bodies when they are active.

P8 Pupils move with some control and co-ordination, *for example they travel under and over climbing equipment.* They follow and imitate sequences and patterns in their movements. They use small and large apparatus safely. They are aware of space, themselves and others. They play simple games and may require support to keep score and follow game rules. They recognise the changes that happen to their bodies when they are active.

Striking and Fielding

Unit of work:	Striking and Fielding
Teaching Group:	Year 10 and 11
	Tuesday P. 8 and 9
Time Allocated:	2.30 p.m. – 3.30 p.m.
	6 x 1hr = 6 hrs

LEARNING OBJECTIVES (Mark key learning objectives with a *)	• To develop and apply more advanced skills • To use more advanced strategies • To be able to apply rules and conventions to different activities • To be able to make informed choices about what role to take • To develop leadership skills • To know how preparation and fitness relate to and affect performance
ASSESSMENT CRITERIA AND ASSESSMENT TASKS – including differentiation	• Improve performances in striking and fielding • To understand why changes in technique improve performance • To be able to act as an official, coach or team manager when others are competing • To be able to take charge of a group of peers and get them to do whatever task is required
LEARNING ACTIVITIES/TEACHING METHODS (chronologically) – including differentiated learning tasks	**Warm-up activities:** Fielding-based pulse raiser. Activity specific stretching. Identify key muscles involved in each activity. How these muscle groups can be prepared for activity and developed **Skill development:** Pupils to research batting, bowling and fielding techniques and rules and then to take the role of coach/official in small groups **Games:** Small competitions based on various striking and fielding games with pupils filling all major roles

RESOURCES needed	<ul><li>Kwik cricket sets</li><li>Batting tees</li><li>Variety of balls</li><li>Variety of bats</li><li>Cones</li><li>Hoops</li></ul>
ROLE OF SUPPORT STAFF	<ul><li>Assist various pupils</li><li>Assist in putting equipment out and away</li><li>Enable pupils to communicate</li><li>Ensure safe practice</li></ul>
CROSS-CURRICULAR (PSE, IT)	**English:** Speaking and listening **Mathematics:** Scoring **Science:** How the body works, warm up **PSHE:** Self-esteem, positive self-concept **RE:** Spiritual: enjoyment of learning. Moral: Consideration of others. Honesty, integrity, turn taking, co-operation **Equal opportunities:** Access for all (see access strategies). Opportunity to play and act as an official **ICT:** Data recording and activity research via the internet

ACCESS STRATEGIES: To establish the optimum roles in striking and fielding games for all pupils and to encourage them to learn the key requirements of each task. Utilise techniques from JSLA to encourage pupils to become good sports leaders. Set up Top Link management teams to utilise the new skills developed and organise sports events.

(copyright © Simon Harris)

Games: Table Cricket

Unit of work:	Games: Table Cricket
Teaching Group:	Year 7, 8, 9 Friday
Time Allocated:	2.00 p.m.–3.00 p.m. 6 x 1 hour = 6 hours

LEARNING OBJECTIVES (Mark key learning objectives with a *)	<ul><li>To prepare for each activity and recover afterwards</li><li>To learn the rules and scoring systems of table cricket</li><li>To develop techniques, tactics and strategies</li><li>To play and compete with positive attitudes, displaying honest competition and good sporting behaviour</li></ul>
ASSESSMENT CRITERIA AND ASSESSMENT TASKS – including differentiation	<ul><li>Warms up for each lesson</li><li>Knows basic rules</li><li>Knows own strengths</li><li>Observes and evaluates others</li><li>Wins/loses graciously; shakes hands with opponents, three cheers, etc.</li></ul>
LEARNING ACTIVITIES/TEACHING METHODS (chronologically) – including differentiated learning tasks	**Warm-Up:** Upper body warm-up based on shake, circle, lift, stretch to involve all arm and hand joints, head, shoulders and trunk. Sometimes to music, sometimes pupils lead. **Table Cricket:**<ul><li>**Bowling:** learning to use fast, spin ball, set the field</li><li>**Batting:** Aiming to score 4's, leave wide balls, learning to avoid the active fielder</li><li>**Fielding:** Practise moving the fielders as directed by the captain Practise being the active fielder</li></ul>**Game:** Play 1 v 1, ability paired, play team v team over a number of weeks<ul><li>Learn to fill in the score sheet</li></ul>

RESOURCES needed	• Coomber and modern music tapes • Table tennis table • Table cricket equipment • Scoring sheets (table cricket) • Table cricket rule book
ROLE OF SUPPORT STAFF	• Act as an official • Assist move fielders (TC) • Assist in putting equipment out and away • Enable pupils to communicate • Record scores
CROSS-CURRICULAR (PSE, IT)	**Equal Opportunities** All pupils take part (see access strategies) **RE** Spiritual: Enjoyment of learning Moral: Consideration towards others Promoting honesty and integrity Cultural: Develop positive self-concept **Maths** Scoring Angles Timing

ACCESS STRATEGIES: All bags removed from the chairs. Tray removed for table cricket. Chest harness removed for table cricket to enable pupil to get closer to the table.

(copyright © Simon Harris)

Accessing Funding

The planning sheet below will help focus funding applications. Many organisations and schemes will look favourably upon applications that meet certain criteria and that are organised in certain ways. Including some sort of development plan alongside the application form may be time consuming, but could make a difference as to whether the application is accepted or not.

1. How does your project meet the funding organisation's key aims and objectives?	These can normally be found either in the information sent with the application form or on the organisation's website. Most funding bodies will also have grants officers who will advise you on such things.
2. How have you consulted the students prior to deciding upon your project to determine their needs?	Showing that the students themselves have been involved in designing the project will give the application added impetus as it shows that you are serious about engaging more children in physical activity. Include the results of surveys with your application.
3. What other key partners have been consulted? What advice have they given?	The support of local representatives of governing bodies of sport, local authority sports development departments, county sports partnerships, clubs, community groups, even prominent local individuals, can be demonstrated by enclosing letters of endorsement with the application.
4. How does your project meet the needs of students? Have specific groups been targeted? If so – why and how?	In the light of a pupil-centred government agenda that seeks to engage more children in sport and utilise physical activity to contribute to child development, this needs to be explained clearly. Applications that target those students not already taking part, or groups who are under-represented locally, regionally or nationally, will often be prioritised.
5. How does your project help the school contribute to local sports development and grass roots sport/physical activity?	In the days of joined-up thinking, projects that dovetail with local sporting networks will be looked upon more favourably than those which simply sit in isolation. Demonstrating awareness of the school's role as devising activity

	which acts as a precursor to their pupils' involvement in community sport, will show funding organisations that you have the capacity to deliver.
6. What national strategies does your project help the school to implement?	Inclusion, PESSCL, Learning Through Sport – there are many sporting strategies that schools are required to implement. Explaining how your project helps deliver these will earn you brownie points with the funders!
7. How does your project contribute to the well-being and development of your local community?	How will participation in your project help the young people involved develop into happier, more conscientious citizens? Will it help them take ownership and feel a part of their community? Will it involve parents and local adults in a way that engenders community cohesion?
8. In what ways does your project allow sport/physical activity to contribute to wider social/educational/ health agendas?	What benefits will the project bring beyond sporting achievement and attainment. The PESS website www.qca.#org.uk/pess has numerous examples of how schools have used physical activity to help meet behaviour and attendance targets, raise self-esteem, encourage healthier lifestyles and improve academic standards. Showing how the project will fit into the school's development plan will seek to convince funding organisations that the school plans to take ownership of the scheme and make it a part of school life.
9. Does your project link physical activity/sport with any other areas?	This could be the arts, environmental projects or even community care. Working with other agencies – health, social services, police – will also demonstrate how your project has a value that goes beyond sport.
10. How many children will benefit from the activities you plan to organise?	Everyone wants to see greater numbers involved in sport and widening participation levels. An application that plans activities in which three hundred children will take part in one activity each is more likely to be looked upon favourably than one which gives 50 children the chance to take part in four. Even better if within the three

	hundred are a substantial number of youngsters who have not previously been involved in physical activity.
11. Who else will benefit from the project?	Will the activities be opened up to children from outside the school or to other members of the community? Will funding allow teachers and other adults to be trained. A community-centred approach is more likely to be successful than a school-centric one.
12. What is your media strategy?	Everybody likes publicity. Showing how you plan to publicise your project locally will help gain you the support of the awarding body, potential partners and, crucially, your head teacher! If students themselves can be involved in the advertising – even better!

Adapted Sports Activities

There are a number of specially adapted activities to use with pupils who have special needs. Some of these are outlined on the accompanying CD:

- Polybat

- Table cricket

- Target cricket

- Zone hockey

- Floor lacrosse

We would like to thank Doug Williamson and the Youth Sport Trust for allowing us to use these. For further information, contact:

Doug Williamson
Nottingham Trent University
Tel: 0115 941 8418 (Ext 3268)
Fax: 0115 948 6626

Youth Sport Trust
Tel: 01509 226600
www.youthsporttrust.org

Polybat (side table tennis) is an adapted form of table tennis devised for people with physical and/or learning disabilities. It can be played with non-disabled partners – sitting or standing.